from generation to generation

D0205112

A MANUAL FOR HEALING

from generation

to generation

A MANUAL FOR HEALING

PATRICIA A. SMITH

Jehovah Rapha Press
P.O. Box 14780
Jacksonville, Florida 32238-1470

Copyright © 1996 by Patricia A. Smith
Cover design and lettering by Lynne Sitton
Photos from the Wood Family Album

Published by *Jehovah Rapha Press*
P.O. Box 14780, Jacksonville, FL 32238-1470

International Standard Book Number: 1-888871-24-5
Library of Congress Catalog Card Number 96-94036

Printed in the United States of America

All rights reserved. No part of this publication may be reproduced, stored in a retrieval system, or transmitted in any form or by any means - for example, electronic, photocopy, recording - wihout the prior written permission of the publisher. The ony exception is brief quotations in printed reviews.

Library of Congress Cataloging-in-Publication Data

Smith, Patricia A.
 From generation to generation: a manual for ministry/Patricia A. Smith

 ISBN 1-888871-24-5
 1. Spiritual Healing. 2. Generational. I. Title.
 235'.4-dc20

Unless otherwise noted, Scripture quotations are from the Revised Standard Version of the Bible, copyright 1946, 1952, 1971 by the Division of Christian Education of the National Council of the Churches of Christ in the USA. Used by permission.

To order additional copies of this book, call or fax: 904-771-3938.
(See back pages for further information.)

This book is lovingly dedicated to my husband, Elston. It would be impossible to list all of the ways in which Elston has loved me, supported me, and enabled me to do this work. Without his quiet sensitivity and patient fortitude it would not have been possible.

Acknowledgments

My deep love and gratitude go to my friend, Christine Atkin, for the many ways in which she helped me give birth to this book. Christine's clear insights and great skill in editing always called me back to the vision that our Lord had given to both of us. Thank you, Chris, for editing, encouraging, and prodding this book into life!

Special thanks to Nancy Moore for the inspiration for the Epilogue, to Julie Nelson for painstakingly transcribing my tapes, and to Susanne Cusick for taking on the hard task of proofreading. Thanks also to friends Minnie Daniels, Laura and Darryl Ingle, Judy and Bob Isaacson, Brenda O'Neill, and innumerable others, for their help and prayers along the way.

My deep gratitude also goes to all those who allowed me to use the stories of their healings in order to help and encourage others in their struggle towards healing and wholeness.

Contents

Introduction 11

Part One: An Introduction to Healing of Generations

One: An Ancient Connection 17
Two: Preparing the Soil 25
Three: Betty's Story: An Illustration: 35

Part Two: Praying Through the Generations

Four: Root Causes of Present-Day Problems 49
Five: The Power of Intercessory Prayer 69
Six: Steps to Healing of Generations 77
Seven: Three Episodes of Generational Healing 105

Part Three: Power for Healing

Eight: The Healing Power of the Holy Eucharist 131
Nine: Deliverance During Healing of Generations 151
Ten: God is Raising an Army! 175
Epilogue 195

Appendixes

A: Genogram 198
B: Renunciation of Occult Practices 200
C: Scriptural Foundations 203
D. Notes 213
E. Recommended Reading 217
F. Book and Tape Order Forms 219

Introduction

Let this be written for a generation to come,
that a people yet unborn may praise the Lord...
Psalm 102.18

This book describes healing of generations - a ministry that God powerfully uses to set people free - in mind, body, and spirit - from the sins and hurts that have come down from the past generations of their family line. People who are active in a ministry of Christian healing are used to having supplicants (those desiring healing prayer) come to them with many difficult emotional problems that have come from their family of origin. In healing of generations prayer, we ask our Lord Jesus Christ to show us where these problems originated in the family line. As we do this, our Lord will often show us that the problem that is bothering the supplicant and his/her family today may have had its beginning generations ago. Ancestors either sinned greatly themselves, or were terribly hurt when they were sinned against by some other person.

In either case, they turned away from God instead of turning to Him for help and did not invite Him into the situation to heal it. Until some family member does this the problems continue to aggravate people in the family line, more and more seriously with each successive generation.

When a family member in the present generation turns to God and asks Him to bring the power of His love and forgiveness into the hurting places in the family line, the painful effects of past sin and hurt are cut off. Then His healing and wholeness can be felt in the lives of present-day family members. Jesus is always our leader and our guide in healing of generations prayer. In the Gospel of John we read,

> Jesus said to them, "Truly, truly, I say to you, the Son can do nothing of His own accord, but only what He sees the Father doing; for whatever He does, that the Son does likewise."
>
> John 5:19

As Jesus said He does only what He sees the Father doing, so when we are engaging in prayer for the healing of a person's generational lines, we are very careful to do only what we see Jesus doing, to go only where Jesus takes us, and to listen carefully and pray only as Jesus would have us pray.

I hope that this short explanation will encourage others to try this ministry for themselves. I especially want to give you, the reader, a guide to enable you to carry on this ministry, and to impress you with the simplicity and effectiveness of the ministry of healing of generations so that you may benefit from it yourself, and also be encouraged to pray for others to receive ancestral healing.

One of the most simple and powerful descriptions of Jesus' ministry was Peter's statement to Cornelius from Acts 10:38:

> ...God anointed Jesus of Nazareth with the Holy Spirit and with power; ...He went about doing good and healing all that were oppressed by the devil, for God was with Him.
>
> Acts 10:38

God hasn't changed. His arm is not stayed nor shortened. He still wants to heal all who are oppressed, especially those who turn to Him through faith in His Son, Jesus Christ.

Today He wishes to empower people for the ministry of healing of generations. There are many who are hurting. There are others whose hearts go out in love and compassion to each hurting soul. Jesus wants to bring these people together, so that His ministry of healing may go on.

With some instruction and experience, anyone whose eyes are firmly fixed on Jesus Christ, and whose heart is moved by His compassionate love, can bring others into healing using the methods taught in this book. Jesus has never failed anyone. According to the promises He has made to those who follow Him, Jesus will always be beside us and will empower us as we venture forth in faith to carry on this new ministry.

Truly, truly, I say to you, the one who believes in me will also do the works that I do; and, in fact, will do greater works than these, because I am going to the Father. I will do whatever you ask in my name, so that the Father may be glorified in the Son. If in my name you ask me for anything, I will do it.

John 14:12-13 (NRSV)

Part 1

An Introduction

to

Healing of Generations

Chapter One

An Ancient Connection

I saw, in a book on Roman Britain, two aerial photographs of the same farm in England taken in the summers of two different years. In the one there was simply the farm (house, barn, fields, a few cattle, walls, gates, hedgerows, and road). It was taken in a year when rain was plentiful, and crops were green.

In the other, taken in a year of drought, there was the farm again, and all that pertained to it; but overlying it, or more accurately, underlying it, and askew of it, now could be seen the clear outlines of an ancient Roman fort, larger than four football fields, with ditches, and walls, and gates, and streets, and barracks, and headquarters. One could almost hear the calls of soldiers, the neighing of horses, the clinking of military gear.

We are more than we seem. We have a history and a form, an ancient connection, the outlines of which we cannot even remember. We live our days, one upon the other, as though our senses accurately assimilate all that we are, or were, or can be. We become accustomed to our now visible form.

Then we are surprised, in some unexpectedly dry season, by an older, deeper, and more elemental self. A self that surfaces willy-nilly, that is not oriented at all to our present-day superimposition. There is ancient recognition, archeological revelation, resolution of past and present, a reunion of the divided self with its ground of being.

This old house has more rooms, more ancient rooms, than the world can count.[1]

This article beautifully describes just what happens in life. We each have 'an ancient connection.' One generation builds upon another. Each individual life is an amalgam of what has gone before. The poet John Donne aptly described this when he wrote, "No man is an island, entire of himself, each is a part of the main."

Only Adam and Eve came into the world without antecedents. Each person who has come after them has had, added to his or her own life experiences, a load of experiences coming down from those who have lived before. Some of those experiences have been good, some have been painful. Some have been helpful and uplifting, others have been crushing and debilitating.

Whether or not our ancestors learned and grew because of the circumstances in their lives or were crushed and devastated by them and passed their pain down to us, all depends on the response they made to each circumstance they found themselves in. If they remained in communion with God by turning to Him for help, if they forgave and were reconciled with those who hurt them, then they passed on peace, love, and understanding to those who came after them.

If they turned away from God and responded with anger instead of understanding, with resentment and bitterness instead of forgiveness, with a desire for revenge rather than a search for reconciliation, then the harvest they passed on was a bitter one, indeed. This is especially so if they turned to some form of pagan worship or occult practice. From such a harvest comes no love, and certainly no hint of peace. A heritage such as this only brings more hurt, more bitterness, more deeply-charged emotion into a family's life. Unfortunately this has been more the rule than the exception in the history of the human race and has come down to us as excess baggage that we neither need nor deserve.

From such a background comes emotional, spiritual, and physical illness, along with personal and social estrangement. It breeds families who have never known accepting, nurturing love, and who cannot free themselves from dysfunctional lifestyles filled with bitter, addictive, incestuous relationships.

We see the results of this running through our society today in broken marriages, in the increase in chemical dependencies, and in the surge of occult and cultist practices. We see it in a modern mind-set which permits and promotes sexual promiscuity, and in the proliferation of sexually-transmitted diseases.

We see it also in the number of hungry and homeless people wandering our streets. These people have been discarded by our society and reduced to total helplessness and hopelessness. They are a strong witness to the fact that the problems we face become successively worse as each generation goes unhealed.

As I said above, these problems were passed down to succeeding generations because of the way people in the generation of origin reacted to them. We are greatly affected by the emotional climate in which we grow up. Our parents' problems are passed on to us simply because we live with them and are the recipients of their emotions, whether good or bad. What we haven't always realized is that often negative emotional and spiritual responses have been in families for many generations, and had as their starting point a traumatic event that happened to the family line at some time back in its history.

"We are more than we seem. We have a history and a form, an ancient connection..." The author of this essay was able to see the ancient ruins lying beneath a twentieth century farm because a lack of rain had dried the fields overlaying it. In just such a way the pain that we feel in our lives today exposes the hurts and problems that have come down through the generations of our families. Many times we do not even know what is wrong, all we know is that our lives are filled with "dis-ease." But God uses our discomfort to get us to seek help for our problems so that He can bring us and our families into healing.

People today are becoming more and more aware of their need to turn to God for the healing they desire. They are in less denial than previous generations were. We are beginning to recognize our

"ancient connection", our "older, deeper, more elemental self."
Now more than ever before, we are doing something about this!
The increasing number of people looking to God for release
through inner healing prayer, counseling, and spiritual direction
testifies to this.

The proliferation of twelve-step programs such as Alcoholics
Anonymous, Adult Children of Alcoholics, Overeaters
Anonymous, Incest Survivors Anonymous, to just name a few, also
clearly shows this. Each of these programs attests to the fact that
today people are struggling to survive the problems that have come
to them from their family of origin. Participants admit that they are
powerless over their particular problem, that only a "Higher
Power" can restore them to sanity, that only as they turn their lives
over to this Higher Power will they find the wholeness they seek.
Today God is using this search for a Higher Power to bring many
people into a knowledge of His saving grace as shown in His Son,
Jesus Christ. There are many hurting people who otherwise would
never have come to know Him and His healing love. These people
find their Higher Power to be Jesus Christ. As they do, they turn
to Him to heal not only their present pain, but also the roots of that
pain that are to be found in the past generations of their families.

People have been hurt deeply and held in bondage to that hurt
simply because they did not know where the problem originated.
Today, through prayer, God is showing us a way to cut off the
effects of generations of dysfunctional living. He is leading us to go
back to that "ancient connection" and bring the healing touch of
Jesus to bear upon it.

God's New Revelation

Several years ago some of us who were working in the ministry of inner healing began to experience a new thing. As we prayed with a person for healing of memories God would sometimes take us back to incidents that the person we were with could not remember. As He did this He would give us the knowledge that this incident was something in the past generations of this person's family that needed to be taken care of before we could go any further with the healing of memories.

The incidents He showed us usually had to do with some trauma that had happened to the family causing them to turn away from God, or some kind of grievous sin that the family's ancestors had engaged in. In each case God seemed to be calling the person with us to intercede for the family members who had sinned in the past, to ask God to forgive them, and to offer forgiveness to them on behalf of present-day family members.

When this first happened to me I didn't know what to make of it. I have a hard time believing some new thing is of God unless there is a definite confirmation of it in Scripture and from other members of the Body of Christ. I also believe that it must work experientially. That is, the fruit of the Spirit must be clearly discernible in it.

The witness I desired came in these three ways:

♦ As I prayed for discernment I began to realize that the basis for this ministry was in the Ten Commandments:

I am the Lord your God, who brought you out of the land of Egypt, out of the house of bondage. You shall have no other gods before me. You shall not make for yourself a graven image, or any likeness of anything that is in heaven above, or that is on earth beneath, or that is in the water under the earth; you shall not bow down to them or serve them; for I the Lord your God am a jealous God, visiting the iniquity of the fathers upon the children to the third and fourth generation of those who hate me, but showing steadfast love to thousands of those who love me and keep my commandments.

Deuteronomy 5:6-8

In almost every case where I was led to pray for the healing of the generations someone had broken this commandment and, by doing so, was guilty of the sin of idolatry. Some of the incidents the Lord showed me involved people in past generations who had sinned greatly and passed the painful results of that sin down through the family line. There were times when a person's ancestors had deliberately turned away from the Lord God Almighty to worship other gods. At other times a great trauma befell the family, causing the people involved to turn away from God and make their hurt the focus of their lives.

However it happened, something had replaced God in their hearts. Whenever we turn from God, we turn towards something else. Whether the thing we turn to is anger, unforgiveness, or grief, it becomes the focus of our lives. Whatever our lives center on becomes our god. This amounts to idolatry. Idolatrous action removes us from the circle of God's protective love. The results of this idolatrous action may plague our progeny for generations to come.

♦   It wasn't too long before word came to me that other Christians were praying in this way. About six months after my first experience of praying for past generations, I attended a conference where one of the leaders told about a strange new phenomenon called "Healing of Generations". Others soon began to testify to the Lord leading them in this type of prayer. A few years later an English Psychiatrist, Dr. Kenneth McAll, wrote a book, *Healing The Family Tree*, about his experiences in this ministry detailing the healing his patients received when he was led to have a priest celebrate a Eucharist for their ancestors.

♦ In Galatians 5:22 St. Paul tells us that the fruits of the Spirit are love, joy, and peace. I saw these fruits in the lives of the people I prayed for every time I did the healing of generations with them. These incidents taught me that noticeable change would occur in the person I was praying with and in one or more family members after we had done healing of generations on their behalf. This satisfied my third requirement.

I now knew that this was not just something happening in some obscure corner of the Church, but simply the newest part of God's continuing revelation. The healing of generations is but one part of the ministry of healing our Lord Jesus Christ left to His Church. His people had to first recapture the significance of His desire and His power to heal the sick and the brokenhearted before He revealed this to them.

This powerful ministry is being raised up in many different places in His Church today. Why is this so? Because God has planned it this way! He has always been in the business of healing His people. He wants them healed of *all* of their hurts: physical, emotional, and spiritual.

Because God wants His people to know His peace in their hearts, He is showing us the barrenness of our 'ancient connection.' He is cleaning out the ruins from under the present-day structure and building a new family structure, that only He can provide, on a foundation of true faith, forgiveness, and love. So many people today cannot even begin to hear His call to them because of the dysfunctional family systems they grew up in. God is offering them this way to wholeness. It is part of His plan of salvation. It is the work of His Church!

Chapter Two

Preparing the Soil

And when a great crowd came together and people from town after town came to him, he said in a parable: "A sower went out to sow his seed; and as he sowed, some fell along the path, and was trodden under foot, and the birds of the air devoured it. And some fell on the rock; and as it grew up, it withered away, because it had no moisture. And some fell among thorns; and the thorns grew with it and choked it. And some fell into good soil and grew, and yielded a hundredfold." As he said this, he called out,"He who has ears to hear, let him hear."

And when his disciples asked him what this parable meant, he said, "To you it has been given to know the secrets of the kingdom of God; but for others they are in parables, so that seeing they may not see, and hearing they may not understand. Now the parable is this: The seed is the word of God. The ones along the path are those who have heard; then the devil comes and takes away the word from their hearts, that they may not believe and be saved. And the ones on the rock are those who, when they hear the word, receive it with joy; but these have no root, they believe for a while and in time of temptation fall away. And as for what fell among the thorns, they are those who hear, but as they go on their way they are choked by the cares and riches and pleasures of life, and their fruit does not mature. And as for that in the good soil, they are those who hearing the word, hold it fast in an honest and good heart, and bring forth fruit with patience.

Luke 8:4-15

When we do healing of generations we are "preparing the good soil," so those who hear the word may "hold it fast in an honest and good heart, and bring forth fruit with patience."

I am a farmer's daughter, and the Parable of the Sower really speaks to me. One of the good things that has come down in the generations of my family is a love of gardening. I delight in seeing things grow in my garden! However, the soil in my yard does not lend itself to gardening very easily. It is filled with rocks and no matter how many times I clear out the rocks there are still more the next time I try to plant. Sometimes I think I am better at growing rocks than any other crop!

Besides the rocks we have wild onions growing in our yard. You should come over and smell them when my husband mows the lawn. We also have thistles. The birds love them! We have a meadow full of wild flowers at the edge of our lawn, and the finches fly in every afternoon at about five o'clock to feed on the thistle seeds. It is a beautiful sight, and I am glad the thistles are in the meadow to attract the birds. But do they have to blow over into my yard? They are impossible to keep out of my garden, and every time I weed I nurse a sore finger because of the thorns on the thistles. Not to mention the fact that we can't walk around our yard in our bare feet because of them.

If I want to have a garden, I first have to contend with our rocky and weedy New England soil. I pick out the rocks, and then I pull up the onion and thistle plants, a job I seem to do over and over again. But that's not all, if I want my garden to grow, I still have to put in peat moss and compost to give the soil more density. Then I have to fertilize it, plant my seeds, water them, and continue to weed, if I want to have a good crop.

There is no way around it, preparing the soil in order to bring forth a good crop is not easy. It demands determination, perseverance, and a lot of real hard, sweaty work. God put into place every thing I would need in order to have a fruitful, productive garden, but I still have to do my part in order for it all to work together properly.

So it is with the healing of our families' hurts. It is not easy work. It takes determination, perseverance, and a lot of real hard labor on the part of the people who wish to have their family problems healed. In doing healing of generations we are asking Jesus to go back into the past and take out the rocks and weeds and brambles which have caused our families to act out their hurts and needs in dysfunctional ways.

We prepare the soil, asking Jesus to expose and heal all of the hurt, pain, and sinfulness that is blocking God's redeeming, life-changing love from flowing through the generational lines. We watch Jesus as He works in an abundant amount of forgiveness and compassion. With God's grace-filled help the bad ways of acting and reacting to one another that have come down through the family line are changed. Then we, and the other members of our families, can hold God's love "fast in an honest and good heart, and bring forth fruit with patience."

As I said before, this is not easy. It is very painful to go back into the hurting and sinful situations in our families' past. But, as anyone who has received this type of healing can witness, it is well worth the pain endured! Just as the gardener has a delicious and bountiful crop to show for the labor, so the people who go through the hard work required to heal the hurts of generations of family members find they have beautiful results to enjoy.

A New Way to Heal Great Hurts

I started to do healing of the generations because as I prayed with people for healing of memories I found that some who came to me with great problems were not being brought into complete healing. These were usually people who had come from extremely dysfunctional homes with very hurting, abusive parents. I began to see that healing the hurting memories of these people was not enough. Their inner pain was only cured as I asked Jesus to send his healing love back into the hurts coming down through their generational lines. And so I began to make this a regular part of the prayers for each supplicant.

I would ask Jesus to show me how to bring healing to the entire family system of each person who came to me. I knew this would only be accomplished as the family member I was working with was able to acknowledge the pain coming down through the family line and begin to work it through with the help of Jesus.

Total healing would only come as Jesus revealed to the victim why the perpetrator had acted in such an abusive manner. With this deep inner knowledge, that only the Holy Spirit can give, would come an ability to forgive the perpetrator. At first the forgiveness was on the level of the will. The person who had been hurt would forgive the abuser as an act of his or her will. After more healing prayer, however, most people would be able to forgive from the heart.

So we would go into prayer asking Jesus to heal a specific hurting memory in this person's life and when He had brought it into healing, we would then ask Him to show us why the perpetrator had acted in this way. What had caused this person to be so abusive?

As we asked this question Jesus would show us either a great hurt that had happened to the perpetrator, or He would take us back many years to a great trauma that had occurred to the perpetrator's forebears. This trauma had in some way been passed down from one generation to another, until it affected the present generation. Now that a person in the present generation had turned to Jesus for help, His healing and forgiving love was able to flow freely back through all of the generations to heal the source of the hurt.

A Surprising Vision

When I first began to do healing of generations, I had no idea of what was happening, or of what I was supposed to do with what I was experiencing. The first experience of praying for past generations I had was with a young man who came to me for prayer for the healing of a very serious emotional problem. His problem had affected his life for many years, and now was threatening his marriage.

Although I had received training in pastoral counseling, I did not feel I had the ability to even begin to counsel this man. As I uttered my favorite prayer under my breath, "Help!", I began to hear what I felt was God's answer: *"My son did not come to you because of your great skill or your worldly wisdom, he came because he wanted My help. You are only to pray for him, and I will give him the healing he needs."*

So I explained to this deeply hurting man that I did not know how to help him with his pain, but that I would pray for him and ask for God's healing touch on his life. As I did this a picture began to form in my mind of a man and a woman. They were dressed in clothes that made them look like German peasants from the last century. The most distinctive thing about them was that they were dressed completely in black and were surrounded by darkness.

Now I don't know about you, but when I see things like that in my mind I begin to wonder about my sanity. So I handed that vision right back to the Lord. I said to him, "I think I'm imagining things, Lord, but if I'm not, please tell me what to do about these people." As I said this I began to feel that they were ancestors of the man I was praying for and that they had been very heavily involved in occult practices. Somehow the effects of that involvement had been passed down through the generations and were now directly connected to this man's problem.

I still didn't know what to do about this, so I uttered my little prayer again, "Help! Lord, show me what to do now." I began to feel that I should ask the Lord to forgive these people, so I prayed softly in the spirit for them, asking the Lord to forgive them and to release them and their descendants from any bondage they were in due to their disobedience to His laws.

As I did this I saw these two people start to change. The darkness around them began to lift, and the black clothes they were wearing began to change to white. I saw them kneel down in front of Jesus and ask His forgiveness for their sinfulness. I then saw Jesus put His hands on them in a gesture of forgiveness. The entire scene turned to one of dazzling light.

As this happened the man I was praying with gave a deep sigh and said that he felt as though a heavy weight had just been lifted from his shoulders. He looked up at me with his face shining and said, "I know I am healed. I can feel the love of Jesus filling me right now." He then went on to tell me that his mother had been heavily involved in occult practices (seances, use of mediums, palm-reading, etc.) all of her life. He also confided that as a child he had been sexually abused by her. I firmly believe that the prayer I said for his ancestors freed him to be able to tell me these things. I never told the man what I was seeing. I really didn't know how to because I didn't understand what was happening myself. I have since found that people who feel the loving touch of Christ are able to believe in His miraculous powers of healing and are affected by them at much deeper levels than we would normally think possible. I referred this man to a counselor and never saw him again. I don't know what happened to him in the future, but I do know that both he and I were touched at a very deep level by the healing love of our Lord Jesus Christ.

Since that day I have seen people healed of all kinds of emotional, spiritual, and even physical problems through the prayer called the healing of generations. I have seen God taking the rocks, weeds, and brambles out of past generations in a way that frees people to live joyful, Christ-centered lives in the present. He is "preparing the soil." He is freeing His people so that they may know Him, love Him, and serve Him. He is healing them so that they may "bring forth fruit in a good and patient heart."

Confirmation

The most exciting thing about healing of generations is that it works! Within a short time after praying for a family's generational line there is usually some clearly observable change in one or more family members. It is exciting to have someone call me up shortly after a healing session to tell me of the change that they have observed. It is thrilling to see hope come back into the life of one who has been caught up in the throes of a hurting, closed family system.

There are many wonderful examples of this in the case histories of the people who have come to me for help. But, as you can see from the above incident, when I first began to do healing of generations I really didn't know what was going on. Despite the fruits I saw I wondered if it was okay to pray in this way. I began to pray for confirmation that this new way of interceding was truly of God.

Not long afterwards, a young woman came to me for prayer. It was shortly before the Christmas holidays. She was very upset. Her words to me were: "I can't stand to spend another holiday with my mother because she has never been a mother to me. She has been on alcohol and drugs for twenty-five years and she has never tried to get help."

We asked Jesus to show us what was causing her mother's behavior. He showed us generations of addictive, abusive behavior in her family, culminating in the abuse her mother received from her own alcoholic parents. Then Jesus showed us a vision of her mother as a neglected little girl, being physically and emotionally abused by her own mother and father. As we prayed for this hurting child, we saw Jesus go to her and hold her in His arms. We could see that His unconditional, healing love continued to flow into her until she was completely transformed.

Two weeks later my friend received a phone call from her mother. These were her exact words: "I must talk to you. I want to ask your forgiveness. I have never been a mother to you. I have been on alcohol and drugs for the last twenty-five years, and I have just started going to a counselor for help."

Uncanny, isn't it? The mother used the exact wording that the daughter had used when telling me of the problem. The Lord knew that we needed confirmation that this ministry was of Him and He gave it to us in this way. I can cite healing after healing that occurred in just about the same way. All of them were objectively verifiable. Not every one was as much on the target as this mother's words were, but there was a noticeable difference in the behavior of one or more of the family members after the prayers for healing of generations were done.

This is the way it is with healing of generations. There is no way to really explain how this kind of healing takes place. It is a mystical experience. It is pure grace from beginning to end. It is the act of a generous Father, taking place through the loving presence of His Son, Jesus Christ, as one person prays for another, empowered by the Holy Spirit.

It begins when a person seeks help with a desire to be healed of his or her own hurt and break the bondage of the family's past, relying on Jesus to do this. When such a person becomes an intercessor for the other members of the family and turns to our Lord for healing He is always there for them. The hymn, *I Sought the Lord*, states, "I sought the Lord, and afterward I knew he moved my soul to seek him, seeking me..." I really believe that this is so. I am certain that it is not we who turn to Jesus for healing, but Jesus who draws us to Himself.

I firmly believe that today God is preparing the soil of His Church by showing us how to take the rocks, and brambles, and thorns out of the hearts and souls of our families through the ministry called the healing of generations. He is doing this from His compassionate heart, because He has had enough of seeing the suffering of His people, of hearing their cries for help! He is doing this because He loves us and wants us to be whole, and because He wishes to prepare us for the service of His kingdom!

Chapter Three

Betty's Story: An Illustration

The Lord is my Shepherd, I shall not want; He makes me lie down in green pastures. He leads me beside still waters; He restores my soul.

Psalm 23:1,2

So many times as I am praying with a person who has great wounds in his or her life, I think of these verses from the Shepherd's Psalm. The love of our Shepherd, Jesus, shines out from them. He is the One Who cares for us in our need and He is the One Who restores our souls. He did this for Betty. She felt a great need for the restoration that only He could give and she continually turned to Him to fill that need.

Betty's story is a good illustration of the problems we see when people come to us for healing of generations. Throughout her story you will also see the steps we go through as we pray healing of generations prayer for an entire family line.

People ask for healing of the generations for many different reasons. Perhaps the most common problem is a pervasive feeling of fear and inner unrest that stems from low self-esteem. Betty's problems were a good example of this. Betty came from a deeply hurting family. Her father had died when she was very small. Her mother was locked into her own pain and not able to give any emotional nurturing to her children.

Although Betty had achieved success in her profession, and had a loving husband and children, she still had strong feelings of worthlessness and inadequacy. When people praised her work her first thought was, "If they really knew me they wouldn't say that."

Betty had already had a lot of help with her problems. She had gone for psychotherapy and she had healing of memories with a prayer counselor. She led a well-balanced Christian life. But still the old feelings of worthlessness would pop up just when she didn't need them. Why? She began to wonder if there were even deeper hurts that needed to be healed.

It was about this time that she heard about the ministry of healing of generations and came to see me for help. The first thing we did when we met for prayer was to ask Jesus to be present with us and to guide us. We thanked Him for the love He had already shown to Betty by bringing her to Him for healing. We prayed a special prayer of protection for each other and for all of our loved ones. We continued to pray softly in the Spirit until we were aware of His presence with us in a very strong way.

Betty's Genogram

We now began to look at Betty's family tree to see where the problems lay. We took a family history and used a genogram (Appendix A) to diagram it so that we could see at a glance where the problems were in each generation. As we made up the genogram we first filled in the names and ages of Betty's siblings. Then we did the same for her parents and their siblings, and so on up the family tree. After we had done this we began to indicate where the problem areas were.

Some of the problems in her family line were known by Betty, such as the fact that her mother and maternal grandmother were very cold and distant from one another, even though they had lived in the same household since Betty was a small child. There were other problems that she knew nothing about until we began to pray. These are the hidden things that only Jesus can reveal. Usually these are the traumas that have caused the most pain to the family.

But, back to the family tree. We now filled in the hurts and traumas that Betty knew about. Betty felt that the biggest problem was her own low self-esteem. Next to that came her mother's inability to give emotional support or nurturing love to her children. In fact, this seemed to repeat the pattern of her mother's relationship to her grandmother.

As we filled in the horizontal lines between her siblings, we saw a lot of problems. She had an older sister and brother. Each one had multiple physical problems, as had Betty, herself. All of the diseases were those that come from deep inner woundedness, something eating away at the inner being of the one afflicted. We also saw that there were problems with alcoholism and other addictions in the family line.

You Shall Have No Other Gods Before Me

One thing that was noteworthy was the amount of occult activity in the family. As a teenager Betty had been very interested in seances and the use of mediums. She had read many books about them, but had been afraid to do any of this herself. However, she had read her horoscope regularly, played with a ouija board, and developed an interest in extra sensory perception.

Her brother and sister were also very interested in occult and spiritualist activities. They also practiced ESP, and had visited palm readers. They played regularly with ouija boards and did water divining. As with many Christians today, they didn't have any understanding of the fact that when they dappled in the occult they were opening themselves up to extremely evil forces. These forces are only waiting to pull Christians away from God's protection.

As I said before, when we practice idolatry we are moving out of the sphere of God's protective embrace. This is especially so when we engage in occult practices, pagan or satanic worship. This is an extremely evil realm of darkness. Some people do this innocently, not knowing the deep darkness they are exposing themselves to. Unfortunately, the powers of darkness don't care whether it is done innocently or not, they are as destructive to those who are just out to get a thrill or play a parlor game, as they are to those whose intent is evil.

It is interesting that our spiritual ancestors brought a curse on the whole human race just by wanting to eat of the tree that would make them "like God, knowing good and evil". (Genesis 3:5) It is this same knowledge that those who engage in occult activity of any kind are seeking. Whether it is consulting a palm reader, or a medium, or playing with a ouija board, they want to be like God. They want to have the kind of knowledge and power that belongs only to Him!

God has expressly forbidden this:

When you come into the land which the Lord your God gives you, you shall not learn to follow the abominable practices of those nations. There shall not be found among you any one who burns his son or his daughter as an offering, any one who practices divination, a soothsayer, or an auger, or a sorcerer, or a charmer, or a medium, or a wizard, or a necromancer. For whoever does these things is an abomination to the Lord...

Deuteronomy 18:9-12

Because Betty and her family had taken part in some of the things listed in these verses, I had her go through a prayer renouncing any occult, pagan or satanic practices she and her family had engaged in, naming each practice she could remember. At the end of the prayer of renunciation I led her through a renewal of her Baptismal promises because every time she had *turned to* one of these practices she had, in effect, *turned away* from God.

These are the words she used:

In the name of Jesus Christ I renounce any satanic, occult, or pagan practices that I or any other member of my family line may have engaged in. This includes, but is not limited to, the following things... (Name any occult practices you know of, or use those in Appendix B)

After the prayer of renunciation Betty said this prayer reaffirming her Baptismal vows:

I ask Jesus Christ to forgive me and my ancestors for turning away from Him to these evil imitations of His knowledge and power. In a reaffirmation of my Baptismal vows I renounce Satan and all the spiritual forces of wickedness that rebel against God. I renounce the evil powers of this world which corrupt and destroy the creatures of God. I renounce all sinful desires that draw me from the love of God. I turn to Jesus Christ and accept Him as my Savior. I put my whole trust in His grace and love. I promise to follow and obey Him as my Lord. Amen."[1]

Thus Betty first renounced any way in which she or her ancestors had turned away from God to practices which He had expressly forbidden; then she made a new affirmation of faith in Jesus Christ as her Savior and Lord, and reaffirmed her promise to join His fight against "Satan and all the spiritual forces of wickedness that rebel against God."

Now that we had prepared Betty's genogram by diagraming every problem that she could remember, and gone through the list of renunciations to remove anything that would hamper our prayers, it was time to ask the Lord to show us what He wanted to heal first in the generations of her family.

A Time of Healing Prayer

With the genogram in front of us, Betty and I and my prayer partner entered into prayer. We prayed quietly in the Spirit for a few minutes. As we did this Betty couldn't get rid of a feeling of utter worthlessness. It was as though she were not good enough for anything but to be thrown away and abandoned.

As we continued to pray Betty saw in her mind's eye a round circle filled with a dense grey fog. In the center of the circle was what looked like a raw, red, wound. She felt as though this wound were deep within her inner being. Feelings of rejection and abandonment welled up inside of her. We asked Jesus to show her why she had these terrible feelings.

As we did this Betty cried out in pain. She was seeing her mother in the bathroom of her childhood home. Her mother had just found out that she was pregnant with Betty, and she was trying to induce an abortion. The grey mist that Betty was seeing was the inside of the womb, and the raw wound was symbolic of the inner pain she had felt as tiny embryo, experiencing her mother trying to abort her. Jesus gave us an inner understanding that this was the source of her persistent feelings of low self-esteem. To the unborn child this attempted abortion seemed like the ultimate rejection. It had made her feel that she was only good to be thrown away, and had given her a pervasive feeling of worthlessness that had been with her throughout her entire life.

We asked Jesus to be present in this situation with Betty. We thanked Him for the love He had already shown to her by revealing the reason for her deep inner hurt. We praised Him for holding

Betty in the palm of His hand and keeping her safe even from her mother's abortion attempt.

We acknowledged our faith in Jesus' continued care and in the fact that we knew He would answer our prayers and bring Betty into total healing and wholeness. We continued to pray softly in the Spirit until we were aware of Jesus' presence with us in a very strong way, and Betty could see Him in the picture with her mother.

She saw Jesus on the stairwell, calling out for her father to come quickly to the bathroom. She saw her father dash into the bathroom and stop her mother before her abortion attempt could succeed. He seemed to be very aware of her mother's inner state of extreme fear and confusion. He quietly took the instrument from her and then held her tenderly in his arms and comforted her. This was completely in character with the kind, gentle nature of her father, as Betty remembered him from her childhood.

Jesus gave us an understanding that Betty's mother had experienced such pain with her first pregnancy that she was extremely fearful of giving birth again. After that she had attempted to abort every time she had found herself pregnant. She had actually succeeded three times.

Betty now understood why she had such a bad self-image. To that tiny unborn child the abortion attempt was the ultimate rejection. It said to her, "You are worthless. You are nothing but refuse, fit to be thrown away." The sense of rejection and worthlessness that had come into her at one of the earliest moments of her life had taken away any chance she might have had to establish a sound basis for self-esteem in the future.

That is, she would not have had a chance without the healing love of Jesus. Jesus began to restore her feelings of security by showing her how her father had reacted to her. He showed her that each evening after she was born her father would walk around the house, holding her in his arms and crooning to her. He would tell her how her how much he loved her and wanted her. He would whisper to her of God's love for her. As she pictured him doing this she felt the depth of his love for her flowing deeply into her inner being, just as she had already felt Jesus' love flow into her in the inner healing sessions she had experienced earlier.

She knew that her father had welcomed her birth. That to him, at least, she was not worthless or a throw away. Even more than this, she began to feel that he actually cherished her. Then Jesus showed Betty how her older sister had also cared for her and loved her with the tenderness that her mother had not been able to supply, attempting to fill in the difference between the love she had needed and the love that she had received.

The warmth she felt flowing into her inner being while she watched these things happening, and the understanding she gained of her mother's state of mind, enabled her to forgive her mother. She also asked Jesus to forgive her mother for the abortions she had succeeded in committing. (Later we celebrated a Generational Eucharist for these children as described in Chapter 8.)

For the first time in Betty's life she understood that her mother's rejection of her had nothing to do with who she was as a person, but only with her mother's deep inner compulsion and feelings of unreasonable fear whenever she found herself pregnant.

The sins of the fathers ... visited upon the children.

Now that Betty understood where her bad feelings about herself had come from, we asked Jesus to show us where the problems between her mother and grandmother had originated. As we did this Betty began to see a vision of two crying children. They were dressed in clothing that placed them in the middle of the last century. They were in the kitchen of a middle class home. The

Lord led Betty to understand that the little girl was her great-great-grandmother.

As we watched we saw a man and a woman with terrible expressions of anger on their faces begin to physically abuse these two helpless children. We received an inner understanding that this mother and father regularly beat their little boy and girl. It seemed as though Jesus was leading us to understand that they were not able to express any feelings to their mother or father without some kind of angry reprisal over it.

He showed us that the pain and humiliation this little brother and sister received from their parents had caused them to distance themselves from other people throughout their entire lives. They had never received any kind of affirmation as they were growing up, so they turned in upon themselves and became very lonely, withdrawn, hurting people. They were unable to make friends or express their emotions in any way.

The Lord led us to understand that despite this the little boy and girl had both grown up and married, but because of their inner pain they were not able to show affection to their spouses or children. The lack of love and estrangement from family members was passed down through the generations to Betty's grandmother and mother. This was why they were emotionally distant from each other and unable to show affection to Betty and her brother and sister.

Although she tried very hard, Betty felt that she was never able to show her children the love and closeness that she felt within herself and really wanted to offer them. She was not abusive to them, as her ancestors had been to their children, but neither was she able to completely open her heart to them and show them how much they meant to her. It was as though that love was sealed away, deep inside her inner being. No matter how much she tried to express it, she always fell short of her goal.

At this point we asked Jesus to come into the scene where the parents were abusing their children. We felt His anger when He saw the little children being abused. We saw Him come between the children and their parents. We heard Him angrily tell these people that they were not to treat His children in that manner. He went to the children and took them in His arms. He held them for a long, long time, letting His love flow into their bodies to heal their physical pain, and into their hearts and minds to heal their emotional needs. As He did this, we could see everything about them change. Their bodies, which had been held in a stiff, fearful stance, now began to relax. Their faces, which had been pinched and frightened, now softened and they began to shyly smile into His face.

Binding and Loosing

As Betty interceded, asking Jesus to forgive her ancestors, we saw Him go to them and begin to explain what a terrible thing they had done. He told them what a sacred trust it was to be able to have children and raise them. He explained how important it was to love them, and instill in them love for others.

As Jesus spoke, their demeanor softened and they began to repent and ask His forgiveness for what they had done to their children. As they did this Betty began to intercede more strongly for her ancestors, again asking Jesus to forgive them. He seemed to be saying to her, "*I can grant them forgiveness, but can you forgive them for all of the harm they have done to you and your family?*"

When I explained to Betty that by forgiving she was not condoning the action of these people, but actually putting them into Jesus' hands, she was able to forgive her ancestors for their abusive behavior. Then I led her to ask Jesus to forgive her for any way in which she had withheld her love from her own children. As she did this, she felt as if chains were falling from around her body. The chains that had come down from these ancestors were also connected with bondage coming from her mother's and grandmother's inability to show love to her. She shed tears of joy as she felt these chains fall away. We then saw Jesus reunite all of the generations of her family into one large, loving group.

Later Betty told me that from that moment on it was as though a flood of love was released in her inner being. She felt so much love within herself that she was unable to keep from showing affection to her husband and children. They, too, seemed to be released from some inner bondage, and were able to react affectionately without self-consciousness for the first time. What a wonderful Savior we have, that He removes all of our diseases and heals all of our wounds!

Do the visions we see during prayer for the healing of our ancestral hurts mean that the family's past history has been changed? I do not know, but I am certain that the *effect* of those hurts on the family line has been changed by the deep intercessory prayers offered sacrificially by people in the present generation, and by the love of our Lord that has been poured into the ancestral lines. As people in the present generation ask Jesus to begin healing their family's deepest hurts, the flow of His divine love is released into all of the hurting places. It is this flow of love, and the forgiveness that accompanies it, that brings healing.

How people are healed during prayers for the healing of generations is a mystery. It is a mystical experience, one that can't easily be explained. I have learned to trust the Lord and leave the answers to Him. One of the signs that the vision is indeed of Him is that all of those praying will see it together. Each will have some understanding or discernment that together adds up to a total picture.

But in the final analysis, I only know that what we are seeing is from Jesus by its fruits. If the prayer time is followed by healing of a certain problem in the person's life, if there is more peace, joy, and love filling his or her inner being, or if there is a clearly discernible change in one or more members of the family, then I know that what we are seeing is from the Lord. Those are the only criteria I know of by which to judge the validity of anything we do in ministry.

The outcome of our prayers for Betty's family line was immediately evident in her life as she continued to feel great inner peace. It was as though she had experienced an inner adjustment. The feelings of low self-esteem and anxiety that had been present as long as she could remember were now gone. A feeling of well-being had replaced them.

But, healing of generations is not a magical solution to all of the problems a person might have. Bad ways of acting and reacting so often become habitual in a family. It is up to each person to seek the help needed in order to break these habits. Since I am not able to work with each supplicant for a long period of time, I usually refer people to a counselor, a psychotherapist, a spiritual director, and/or an appropriate twelve-step program, depending upon their need.

Betty had already done a lot of work with a counselor and felt that she had received the help she needed in that area. I referred her to a spiritual director whom she began to see regularly. Her guidance helped Betty grow stronger emotionally and spiritually.

She looked for and received support from her Christian friends, who continued to encourage her and pray with her. She felt that her greatest help was a deepened personal relationship with her Lord and Savior, Jesus Christ.

Part 2

Praying

through the

Generational Lines

Chapter Four

The Root Causes of Present-day Problems

Therefore, just as sin came into the world through one man, and death came through sin, so death spread to all because all have sinned.
Romans 5:12 (NRSV)

The history of the human race echoes the pages of the Bible. It shows us that we human beings have constantly struggled with the results of our wayward use of the gift of free will that God bestowed upon us. I remember someone once saying that the only thing we should really be angry at God for was giving us free will. We seem to have a predisposition within us that leads to rebellion against God's laws, and an enemy without who is only too willing to tempt us to break them. From the cradle on up our desire is to have our own way, no matter what harm that independence will bring to us.

The problems we see coming down in our generational lines have to do with this inner predisposition to sin, and with the temptations our ancestors gave in to which came to them from our old enemy, Satan. The Apostle Peter wrote, "Be sober, be watchful. Your adversary the devil prowls around like a roaring lion, seeking someone to devour." (1 Peter 5:8) This certainly seems to have been our ancestor's experience!

Every time they turned away from God to their own ways and did not repent of the evil they had done, every time they were hurt and sinned by not forgiving the people who hurt them, every time they were grief-stricken and blamed God and others instead of working that grief through to resolution, they passed both the effects of their sin, and the pain resulting from their actions, down through their generational lines.

Whenever we turn away from God, we turn to something else. That 'something else' then becomes our god. In *How to Walk with God*, Terry Fullam writes,

> Essentially, whatever concerns us ultimately, whatever is the controlling dynamic of our life, is our god. For some people it's family; for others, careers, or getting ahead and reaching the top. Whatever is dominant in our life is our god; and if it is anything other than the Lord God Himself, that's idolatry.[1]

I have worked with people whose ancestors were extremely angry because of murders that had been committed against a forebear of theirs. These ancestors seemed to be consumed with a desire for revenge against the murderers. Because no one had ever forgiven this great wound a spirit of revenge had run rampant in their family for generations, causing untold emotional and psychological damage. Revenge and unforgiveness had become their gods.

I have prayed for a young woman whose alcoholic father physically abused her, only to have the Lord reveal that her father had been sexually abused by his mother, who was also an alcoholic. When we asked Jesus to reveal why this family had such great problems, He showed us that their ancestors had turned away from Him to occult involvement. The inner pain this alienation had caused was then passed down from generation to generation and became the sole focus of that family's attention, completely replacing God in their lives.

Cleaning out the Attic!

In order to secure a generational healing that is complete in every way we have learned that we must not stop at surface problems, we must continually look for those deep hurts and sins which have caused the people in past generations to turn away from God. A *surface*, or *presenting problem*, is the hurt that brings a person to us in the first place. The surface problem might be something like a family history of alcoholism, uncontrollable anger, sexual abuse, or deep depression. These are all the cause of immense pain, but it has been our experience that they are not the deepest hurt, they are *symptoms* of a *root cause* that lies far back in the family line.

So when we are doing healing of generations, we don't stop at the first floor of the house that represents the generations of a family tree. We go all the way up into the attic, where the worst hurts and sins have been hidden away. These problems may seem to be lost in the dust and mold of generations of familial cover-ups, but Jesus knows what they are and where they are. As soon as a person in the present generation turns to Him for help, He is there exposing those deep, hidden, family hurts and sins with His healing light. And the good news is that everything He reveals He will also bring into complete healing!

So, as we go into healing of generations prayer with a person, we usually find that in every instance where we see a severe problem in the present generation there is an underlying *root cause* that lies far back in the family's history. This root cause has often been the *controlling dynamic* of that family's life for a long, long time and is actually connected to great sins that people in past generations have committed, or great traumas that they experienced that were coming from someone else's sinfulness.

The person we are praying with may tell of problems such as a family history of alcoholism, incest, or broken relationships. As we go to Jesus in prayer asking Him to heal these problems, He may take us back into a hurting memory from the supplicant's childhood, or He may take us back several generations and show us a traumatic incident in the family line that caused much pain. As Jesus brings a picture of the hurting incident into our mind's eye, we ask Him into the situation to heal it. When He has healed that problem, we continue to ask Him to take us back to the root cause, the true beginning of the family's hurt and dysfunction.

As you can see, we ask Jesus to heal each incident He shows us in the same way we would ask Him to heal a hurting memory from our own past. However, in ancestral healing we have to dig much deeper, go back much further, until we find the outstanding hurt or sin that is the 'granddaddy' of them all. So, after He has healed one incident we keep asking Him, "Where did this problem have its beginning?", or "Show us the root cause of this family's pain.", until He has taken us very far back into the past generations of the family line we are praying for. Here we will see a great hurt that happened to someone in the family line, or we will see an ancestor taking part in a great sin. This, then, is the root cause of all of the terrible problems this family has had down through the centuries.

As we watch Jesus, we see Him bring healing into each sinful or painful incident. We receive a deeper understanding of His redemptive power as His unconditional love flows into each hurting person, freeing them from their pain and sin.

There is no way that I can truly say with certainty what is happening when we intercede for the traumas coming down through past generations. It is more than I can fathom. It is pure mystery from beginning to end. Webster's dictionary states that a mystery in theology is "any assumed truth that cannot be apprehended by the human mind."

A Theological Word Book of the Bible defines mystery in this way:

> "In the NT a mystery is a secret which has been, or is being, disclosed; but because it is a divine secret it remains mystery and does not become transparent to men. . . .For Paul *the* mystery relates to the inclusion of the Gentiles as well as the Jews in the divine purpose of salvation (Rom. 16.26f., Col. 1.27, Eph. 3.3-6). This is mystery, not because it offers so little to our understanding, but because its superabundant wealth overwhelms our understanding (Col. 2.2; cf. Phil. 3.8).
> The man of sin (II Thess. 2.7), the scarlet woman (Rev. 17.5-7), the institution of marriage (Eph. 5.32), are all mysteries, because they have a significance in the framework of the divine plan which is made known only by revelation.[2]

In much the same way, healing of generations is a mystery. It is a "divine secret" that is not "transparent" to us. It "overwhelms our understanding" because its "superabundant wealth", which is seen in the outpouring of God's healing power into our family lines, is more than we could ever have asked for, or hoped to receive.

Is what we are seeing fact or symbol? Is past history changed when we pray for our ancestral lines, or is it just the *effect* of that history on the present-day family members that is changed? The answers to these questions remain in the realm of mystery. However, the fruits of peace and love now present in the supplicant after a session of healing of generations prayer show us that spiritual and emotional bondage has been removed from the family line. We never stop our prayer until we know that we have definitely come to this point of healing. We will know we have reached it when the supplicant and the prayer counselors share positive feelings of deep peace and reconciliation. We will also be able to look over the genogram and see that the deepest problems of this family have been healed by this time of prayer.

The Most Prevalent Root Causes

In almost every case we have worked with, Jesus has shown us that the root cause of generational problems usually lies in one of five different categories that we see over and over again in this ministry:

♦ **Occult involvement, pagan or satanic worship.**
♦ **Unresolved grief.**
♦ **Unforgiveness and bitterness.**
♦ **Possession-bondage.**
♦ **Violent or early deaths, suicides, or abortions.**

Occult Involvement, Pagan or Satanic Worship

The most difficult situations come when someone in the past generations has turned away from God to some form of idolatry. This may be in the form of idolatrous worship, as when we see ancestors engaged in pagan or satanic worship, or some kind of occult activity. This is the most grievous sin because many of these rituals involve turning away from God to sinful rituals which include human sacrifice, bestiality, and other extremely sinful actions.

This is the most prevalent problem and the most harmful to the family line. It is in direct disobedience to the commandment quoted in Deuteronomy 5:7: "You shall have no other gods before Me." This kind of action involves making a definite decision to turn away from the Lord God Almighty to worship a false god. This may result in curses being put on the families who engage in it, and on their innocent victims.

I have had person after person come to me locked in the pain that comes from incestuous abuse. Time after time the Lord has lead us back in the family line to the place where some ancestor had been involved in pagan or satanic worship. These are the sins which cause the most hideous consequences to come down in the family line.

There may be occasions when there are different root causes for problems such as incest, but my experience has been that the worst problems I see come from an ancestor who has deliberately turned away from the Lord God to the worship of some kind of false god. From this sinful activity, which totally alienates one from God, flow further sins such as bestiality, incest, rape, and murder. It leads to diseases such as alcoholism and other forms of chemical dependency. It promotes emotional, psychological, and spiritual breakdown through the gradual disintegration of the personality. It is only when a person in the present generation of the family turns back to God in faith and intercedes for the past generations that the bondage coming from this curse is broken.

Remember the warning God gave to His people:

> You shall not make for yourself a graven image, or any likeness of anything that is in heaven above, or that is on the earth beneath, or that is in the water under the earth; you shall not bow down to them or serve them; for I the Lord your God am a jealous God, visiting the iniquity of the fathers upon the children to the third and fourth generations of those who hate me, but showing steadfast love to thousands of those who love Me and keep my commandments.
>
> Deuteronomy 5:8-10

This warning against pagan worship and idolatry is repeated in at least five different places in the Bible. (Exodus 20:5-6, 34:7, Numbers 14:18, Deuteronomy 7:9, Jeremiah 32:18) God wanted to impress very strongly on the minds of His people the seductive power of idolatry. The Lord God Almighty is a holy God! He cannot live in communion with a people who engage in unholy practices. People who turn away from God to witchcraft, satanic or pagan practices take themselves outside of His realm and actually bring upon themselves and their progeny the curse that is stated in these verses. The same thing happens to those who will not turn to God for healing of their grief, or who harbor unforgiving, revengeful, bitter thoughts in their hearts and minds.

Whether this is done innocently or deliberately, the outcome is the same. The people who do these things cut themselves off from God. They remove themselves from the protection that His presence affords them. Satan and his minions then have easy access to them. He continues to harass them until one sinful action leads to another, and the effects of their iniquity continue to plague their families for generations to come.

It is not possible for any human being to atone for the unholy practices of the people in ages past. But, thanks be to God that He sent His Son, Jesus Christ, to atone, to pay the price for the sin of the world. Jesus' death upon the cross did, indeed, pay the price for your sin and for my sin, and for all of the sins that our ancestors committed in ages past and that our progeny will commit in times to come.

Unresolved Grief

Unresolved grief also causes great problems to come down in the family line. I am not speaking of the grief that comes to a person who has suffered a loss and is in the process of working it through to resolution. What I am referring to is grief that is not worked through to resolution, grief that is held onto after a very painful loss, because a decision not to let go of it has been made either consciously or unconsciously. This decision causes a person to turn away from God and from other people in order to nurse the anger and hurt they feel.

Unresolved grief carries with it an inner core of anger toward the person who is thought to be responsible for the loss; whether that is the person who has died or another person (such as a person who was driving the car in a fatal accident). The unforgiving mourner usually feels great anger toward God because they feel that God could and should have kept the loss from occurring. Thus it, too, fits into the category of unforgiveness.

Unforgiveness and Bitterness

Unforgiveness and bitterness cause a spirit of revenge to take root in a person's heart and this, in turn, affects all of the people around that person. People who hold onto revenge turn away from God because they cannot be in communion with God when holding onto bitter, vengeful thoughts! Where there is unresolved grief, and an unforgiving, vengeful spirit, there is no room for God. These emotions take on a life of their own and twist our nature into an ugly caricature of what God intended it to be. This spills over into the lives of all of those near to us, hurting them and many times infecting them with the same spirit of bitterness and vengeance.

I have had people come to me filled with a desire for revenge that had been passed down, generation to generation, by forebears who had never forgiven a wrong done to them. The people who come to me don't even know why inner feelings of bitterness and anger have such a strong hold on them. They have lived with negative emotions for so long they don't have any idea what it would be like to be at peace. These emotions fill their minds in such a way that they actually take over their lives and become gods to them. This, too, amounts to idolatry, because the desire for revenge has become the center of their lives. As I said before, God is supposed to be the center of our lives and anything that takes His place becomes an idol to us.

The people who nurture unforgiveness and resentment may be led into inner vows and/or bitter root judgements. An *inner vow* is a vow set early in life by someone who has been grievously hurt, usually by the actions of some other person. A person who was deeply hurt by someone they trusted might vow, "I'm never going to let anyone get close to me again."

A *bitter root judgment* is very much like an inner vow. It is usually a judgment against a certain person or group of people, such as a man making a judgment that all women are after his money or a woman teaching her daughters that men can't be trusted. These vows and judgments will pass down through the generations from person to person in a family line. Each person who holds them will feel justified in doing so. This is because inner vows and bitter root judgments seem to take on a life of their own, just as curses do.

In *Transformation of the Inner Man* John and Paula Sandford point out that inner vows and bitter roots are subject to the *law of sowing and reaping*. This means that when you expect people to act badly toward you, you set into effect a spiritual law that actually causes the thing you expect to happen. So if there is a history of husbands being absent when they are needed at home coming down through the generations of a family, there also may be a bitter root judgment that "you can't trust men, they won't be there when you need them." This attitude of mistrust then sets up a condition that practically fulfills the expectation.

I saw this most recently in a woman who totally mistrusted men. Her father was an alcoholic who emotionally abused her. Her grandfather had sexually abused her mother. She was afraid of men and she was extremely angry at them. I am sure that she had good reasons for her feelings. The difficult thing was that her husband was being terribly hurt by her attitude. He couldn't understand what he had done wrong, and in his hurt he began to fulfill her bitter-root expectations.

I was sure that the problem had originated in the past generations, although it was playing itself out in the present. She did not want to hear this. She felt she was justified in holding on to her anger and feelings of betrayal. She certainly had reason to be angry at her father, but her husband was not the guilty party.

I persuaded her to have patience while we asked the Lord to show us what the problems were back in the generations of her family. As we did this, He took us back to her great-grandmother's childhood. Jesus showed us that this woman's mother had died when she was a young girl. As a very young girl she had become responsible for her younger brothers and sisters.

She was very angry at her father for putting this burden on her and not helping with it. But the most painful thing was that while she was still very young he arranged a marriage for her with a friend who was more than twice her age. When she was sixteen, he made her marry an older man she did not even like.

She fought and fought with her father, but to no avail. He locked her in her room until time for the wedding. Then her new husband took her off to his home to live and work much as she had since her mother had died. This led to an inner vow that men would never control her life again, and the bitter root judgments that men will always betray you, and that no man can ever be trusted. As soon as she was able to she left her husband and children and ran off to live in another city. But she left a legacy of bitterness and unhappiness that came down through the generations to the present day.

As Jesus showed us these things her great-granddaughter, the woman I was praying with, realized how she had given in to the same tendency to make inner vows and bitter-root judgments. As this happened, I led her to renounce them and declare them null and void in Jesus' Name. She forgave her grandfather and great-great-grandfather on behalf of all of the members of her family line and this action immediately brought her great relief.

In the pamphlet, *Jesus Heals Our Childhood Vows*, Phoebe Cranor has this to say:

> Apparently such childish resolves are emotional, made not out of rational thought, but out of the necessity to somehow protect ourselves from hurt. Because they are so hidden in our depths, we do not realize they are there. Yet we keep them as diligently as if we had signed our names in a big black book. They influence our behavior without our knowing why we do the strange things we do, until continuing prayer and growth in the Lord's ongoing plan brings them to light. If we are puzzled by any of our instinctive behavior, we might do well to pray for some light on an old pledge dictating our actions.[3]

I look for inner vows, and bitter root judgments and expectations, when there seems to be a hardened attitude that won't give way during the time of prayer. This often brings with it a desire for revenge, but this should be gone after Jesus has healed the hurts in the past generations. If it is not, you can be sure that the root cause has not yet been found and you must continue to ask Jesus to lead you to it.

Possession Bondage

In *Healing the Family Tree*, Dr. Kenneth McAll, a British psychiatrist, documents cases of disturbed patients who were suffering from what he describes as *'possession syndrome'*. That is, the patient was in some kind of spiritual or emotional bondage to another person.

Dr. McAll writes,

> A relationship between two people, begun happily and voluntarily on both sides, may reach a point at which one partner becomes passive and totally dependent upon the other. Frequently the passive partner is unaware of the loss of his own identity and eventually is completely

unable to break away from the other's control. This state has been termed 'the possession syndrome'.

It is essential to make a differential diagnosis in each case and to classify the possession syndrome into one or more of the defined categories. The bondage of the living to the living is the most obvious to diagnose. The bondage of the living to the dead, whether to ancestors, to those not related, to stillborn, aborted or miscarried babies, or to those who once inhabited a particular place now occupied by the living, can present considerable difficulties in diagnosis. The bondage of the living to occult control is, perhaps, the most dangerous evil to unravel.[4]

Dr. McAll teaches that deliverance from this kind of bondage is a process, not a "one-step miracle pill to be swallowed on impulse for an instant cure." He states that it is necessary to:

...cut the known bond to the living, controlling person or the curse by the dead, controlling person, then to forgive wholeheartedly, finally, to transfer control to Jesus Christ, making any essential environmental changes to support these steps."[5]

Dr. McAll presents case histories showing that many of his patients were healed of very serious emotional disturbances when he had a Eucharist celebrated for their ancestors. During the Eucharist the patient would pronounce the ancestor forgiven and commit the ancestor into Jesus' hands. The bondage of the living to the dead was broken in the Name of Jesus Christ and then the control of the living person was transferred to Him. In each instant the disturbed person was completely well after the Eucharist was celebrated.

To Christ has been given the care of the controlling spirit and to Him must be given the total care of the life that is no longer being controlled.[6]

When I first read Dr. McAll's book, I was ministering to a young woman named Jennifer who had suffered many deep inner wounds. She had grown up in an extremely troubled family. There was a high incidence of alcoholism, incest, suicides, abortions, and occult involvement throughout her family. She also suffered from the disease of alcoholism.

Fortunately for Jennifer, she was led to Alcoholic's Anonymous where she found sobriety. Eventually, as she searched for a way out of the pain in her life, she asked Jesus Christ to be her Higher Power. Christian friends began to pray for her. When she began to attend church, she came to me for help in unraveling the bondage she had been in. Because of her willingness to do the hard work that would lead to total healing, Jesus was now cutting off the last of the heavy chains of bondage coming down from centuries of idolatrous behavior through the healing of generations.

Jennifer was very open to prayer counseling and had already received a great deal of healing before I read Dr. McAll's book, but we both felt that there was some kind of bondage that she was still afflicted with. We decided to celebrate a Eucharist for the express purpose of releasing both the living and the deceased members of her family line from any possession-bondage they might be in.

As we did this, we experienced a strong sense of the Lord's presence with us and of His involvement with the deceased members of her family. He showed us the oppression they had been under ever since a forebear had become involved with satanic worship. A predisposition to satanic involvement had been passed down through each generation of her family, and was directly responsible for the families debilitating problems.

The Lord revealed to us that an aunt, who was involved in witchcraft, had actually cursed Jennifer while she was still in her mother's womb, so that she would be the one in the present generation to carry on the satanic and occult involvement. This curse had actually caused possession bondage between Jennifer and her aunt.

As we celebrated the Holy Eucharist for her family line, Jennifer told me that she felt as if she were completely bound up with heavy iron chains. A symptom of this curse was that throughout her life she had suffered a recurring dream in which she saw witches on broomsticks coming to pull her from her bed. Her aunt was always at the head of the pack.

We declared the curse that her aunt had placed on Jennifer and her bondage to her aunt broken in Jesus' name. Jennifer forgave her aunt and asked Jesus to forgive her aunt. She then asked Jesus to take control of her life. As this was done, she felt the chains binding her beginning to break. (It has been ten years since this time of prayer and the dream has never returned.)

However, she still didn't feel completely free. She felt as though there were still some bondage left. We asked Jesus where this feeling was coming from. He reminded her that ever since childhood her mother had controlled her, even to the point that she felt that her mother could read her mind and that she had to tell her mother everything she was thinking. Now she felt as if there were a part of her mother inside of her, a '*mother-spirit*' taking over part of her very being.

Jesus showed us that this, too, was possession-bondage. We again went through the steps of declaring this bondage to her mother broken in Jesus' Name. Jennifer then forgave her mother and asked Jesus to forgive her. Then we transferred the part of Jennifer that had been in bondage to her mother into Jesus' hands. As this happened, Jennifer saw Jesus reach out to her and pull her into His arms in a gesture of love and protectiveness. Shortly after this, Jennifer's father died and her mother tried to persuade her to live with her. Because Jennifer was now free from the possession-bondage to her mother, she was able to tell her that this would be a bad idea for both of them. Surprisingly, after a while her mother accepted this graciously, something she would never have been able to do before. Since that time her mother has become an active Christian and has developed an interesting life of her own. We feel certain that it was the prayers and the Holy Eucharist of the Generations that was celebrated for Jennifer's freedom from possession-bondage that made the decisive difference.

The Uncommitted Dead

Great inner pain can be found in a family line where people have died without being committed into the Lord's hands. This is especially true where there have been violent deaths, suicides, or miscarried, aborted, or stillborn babies in the family line. When these have not been properly committed into the Lord's hands a celebration of the Holy Eucharist needs to be held for this purpose. Dr. McAll also speaks to this:

I have over six hundred recorded cases of direct healings which have taken place after a Eucharist has been celebrated for babies - who were either aborted, miscarried, stillborn or discarded at birth and who had never been loved or properly committed to Jesus Christ in a burial service. When a Eucharist has been held for such infants, the results have been startling. Many have felt the benefit of the healing power that was generated including patients who were actually taking part; patients who were miles away in hospitals and mental institutions and knew nothing about the services; and even disturbed relatives in foreign countries.[7]

A feeling of illegitimacy, or not having the right to live, sometimes overtakes people whose parents lost a child before they were born, especially if they had been given the same name as the dead child. As soon as the Eucharist is celebrated for the deceased these feelings are gone. I have conducted similar Eucharists for aborted or stillborn babies, and for those who have died violent deaths or committed suicide. In each case there was a clearly observable healing in the person being prayed for after the Eucharist had been celebrated.

An example of this kind of problem was a man who came to me because of a life long history of depression. He was in his forties when he came to me, and he told me that all through his life he had felt as though he was living in a shadow. It was as though he was living his life for another person. When I took his history he told me that he had a twin who was stillborn. I immediately saw the need to celebrate a Eucharist for his stillborn twin brother in order to commit him into the Lord's hands. After the Eucharist was celebrated, this man felt immediate relief of his depressive feelings. They have never returned.

I have had women come to me in great inner pain because they have not been able to experience peace ever since they had an abortion performed many years before. After a Eucharist was celebrated to commit the aborted infant into Jesus' hands, each mother was able to see her child with Jesus. Each one of them saw her child at the age he or she would now be, had the child not been aborted. Each of these women spoke of experiencing an inner peace they had not known since the time the abortion took place. I have had others come for healing and not experience it until they told me of abortions or stillborn babies, or relatives who had died violent deaths, back in the generations of their family.

A woman with this type of problem was Alice, who could never see Jesus as I led her through prayers for healing of generations. I finally realized the problem - her mother had suffered through three miscarriages and a set of stillborn twins. I celebrated a Eucharist for all of these children, and also for her father, who had committed suicide.

The next week Alice returned with a more recent problem. She had been greatly hurt by something a friend had said to her during the week. I suggested she close her eyes and see herself back in the restaurant where she had been lunching with her friend when the hurtful remark was made. Then I asked her to describe what she was seeing. She described herself sitting across from her friend in a restaurant booth. I said, "What is Jesus doing?" She answered, "He's sitting next to her and telling her she should be more loving to her friends." From that moment on, she was able to see Him clearly each time we prayed. In some way her ability to see Jesus had been blocked by the need to commit her deceased siblings and her father into God's hands. Now that this had been done, she felt a spiritual freedom that she had not experienced before.

A Walk Toward God or Away From Him

Alice's story is a good example of what happens when there are deep hurts and sins in the past generations of our family lines. In some way they keep us from seeing Jesus clearly and knowing Him as He truly is. Jesus wishes to have a deep, abiding, loving relationship with each one of us. His greatest desire is to have us understand this.

However, so often it happens that we and our ancestors have turned away from His love to something which is only a poor substitute. This counterfeit too often succeeds in pulling us away from His love, instead of taking us to Him. I have often thought of our old adversary, Satan, as being like a door-to-door salesman. He is just waiting for us to open the door a little bit, so that he can get his foot in it. From that moment on, Satan will keep tempting us to do things that will turn us away from Jesus, until he has successfully completed the task of separating us from Him forever.

The root causes we see in the past generations of our families came from times when he almost succeeded. That he did not succeed entirely, is shown by the fact that Jesus has chosen today to heal the people in the present generation, no matter how sinful the actions of their ancestors might have been.

This tells us that even though we have been hurt by the sins in our ancestral lineage, we are not pre-programmed by them. Each of us has been given free will by a loving God who wishes us to turn *to* Him out of love and desire, and not *away* from Him out of fear and anxiety. Each one of us has the same decision to make: to either walk toward God or away from Him.

When people in the present generation turn to God in love, seeking a relationship with Him through His Son, Jesus Christ, the Holy Spirit will put a longing in their hearts that will help them to choose the right way. He will guide them along the path and keep them from stumbling until they are totally united with Jesus. Praise God for His incredible love!

Chapter Five

The Power of Intercessory Prayer

The Transformation of Time

> But do not ignore this one fact, beloved, that with the Lord one
> day is as a thousand years, and a thousand years as one day.
>
> 2 Peter 3:8

Engaging in prayer for the healing of generations has strengthened my belief that we actually live in two dimensions at the same time, one made up of material reality and the other of spiritual reality. At the same time that we are 'at home' in the world of material things, we are also living in this world of unseen, or spiritual reality. The world of material reality is made up of time and space, of houses, and cars, and people. The world of spiritual reality does not rely on any of these things. Rather its reliance is on the love of God, the redemptive work of Jesus, and the empowerment of the Holy Spirit.

Time is also different in the spiritual world. *Chronos,* or chronological time, as we know it, is only a device God has given us to keep order in the created realm. To God, time is all of one piece. With Him past events do not belong to yesterday alone, they are also part of the ever-present moment, the 'eternal now'. God sees all of time in just the same way we would see the terrain below if we were looking down from a great height, as we do when we climb a tower, or soar high in an airplane. From this great height we would see a wide-angled view of the whole countryside at one glance, with all of the houses, trees, lakes, and people included.

In just this way, God sees time, as though all of time - past, present, and future - were part of one terrain. Included in that terrain would be every person who had ever been part of our lives, whether deceased or still living. Also included would be every event in our personal history, whether past, present, or future. The most important moment in that history would be *kairos*, the right moment. This is the moment when it is expedient for God to act on our behalf. Every time that we approach God, whether for forgiveness, for intercession, or for worship, is kairos. This is the opportune moment for us to bring ourselves and those we pray for into an encounter with God and His healing love, through the person of Jesus Christ.

As Jesus answers our prayers, chronos becomes kairos, our time changes into God's time, and His healing touch is brought into the painful situation. The outcome of this transformation of time is that the yoke of oppression coming from past generations is unbound. This allows Jesus' healing power to flow into people in the present generation and release them and their progeny from the painful effects of past hurts.

Whether we acknowledge it or not, we become part of this spiritual world, with its God-focused understanding of time as soon as we become followers of Christ Jesus. Whenever we pray, whether for ourselves or for others, we enter this spiritual kingdom. When we worship, and most especially, when we partake of the Holy Eucharist, we are in this spiritual realm in a very powerful way. In this realm all of the promises of God are already realized and we have all of the power and authority that God has so graciously promised to all of His people.

Heavenly Warfare

And between the throne and the four living creatures and among the elders, I saw a Lamb standing, as though It had been slain, with seven horns and with seven eyes, which are the seven spirits of God sent out into all the earth; and he went and took the scroll from the right hand of him who was seated on the throne. And when he had taken the scroll, the four elders fell down before the Lamb, each holding a harp, and with golden bowls full of incense, which are the prayers of the saints . . . And I heard every creature in heaven and on earth and under the earth and in the sea, and all therein, saying, 'To him who sits upon the throne and to the Lamb be blessing and honor and glory and might for ever and ever!' And the four living creatures said, 'Amen!' and the elders fell down and worshiped.

Revelation 5:6-8,13-14

When we do healing of generations we are engaging in intercessory prayer for all of the generations of the people in a family line. We are asking God to take us back to the very womb of this family, back to the places where all of the pain and hurt had their birth. In order to do this, we enter into an intense and powerful form of petition. As we do this, we must never lose sight of the fact that we are never alone. We are engaging in heavenly conflict. We are with Jesus before the throne of God, and He has already won the battle. At the same time, we must be sure that we do not stop praying until we have seen the results of that victory in the lives of those we are interceding for.

Jesus willingly gave His life to pay for our sins and the sins of our ancestors. He now willingly brings us all of the healing we need and desire. It is He who intercedes with us day and night before the throne of God!

In *Prayer: Key to Revival*, Paul Y. Cho states,

In intercession, the Christian enters into the priestly function of providing an earthly base for God's heavenly interests. This age has become the battleground between the two opposing forces, but God has a group in the foreign land that is able to bring the influence of the age to come into this age. Therefore, this natural world can be brought under the obvious control of the kingdom of God.[1]

In the Epistle to the Ephesians we read,

> God, who is rich in mercy, out of the great love in which he loved us ... made us alive together with him, ... and made us sit with him in the heavenly places in Christ Jesus.
>
> Ephesians 2:4-6

It is from this vantage point that we begin our prayers for healing of the generations. It is because we know that God has already won the battle in heaven and has given us the spiritual authority to complete the conflict on earth, that we even dare to begin praying for the person who has come to us. For intercessory prayer is a time of battle when we storm the very gates of heaven to bring the person we are praying for before the throne of God.

As we see depicted in the fifth chapter of the Revelation to John, there before the throne stands the Lamb, He who was slain before the beginning of the world, He whose blood paid the price for our sins and the sins of the whole world. Falling down before Him and worshiping Him are all the heavenly court, and in their hands are "golden bowls full of incense, which are the prayers of the saints" (Revelation 5:8).

Our prayers are joined with worship rendered to the Lamb and through Him ascend to the Father. In effect, we are there with all of the hosts of heaven standing before the throne of God day and night. Through the blood of the sacrificial Lamb of God we are allowed presence into the very courts of heaven. God has "raised us up with Him, and made us sit with Him in the heavenly places in Christ Jesus . . . " (Ephesians 2:6).

This is very important for us to remember, for it is not an easy thing we do when we begin this ministry. We are taking part in prayer that will break the back of bondage that has been keeping whole families enslaved for many, many years. We cannot do this on our own strength alone! It is done only through the grace of God, and only through His strength and power. *He is always with us when we ask Him to be and it is His greatest desire to free His people through this ministry.*

We need to honor this and learn to rely on Him completely, *but* we also need to remember that He is relying on us to carry out His work in this world.

In the classic, *Courage to Pray*, Anthony Bloom writes,

We often intercede. We pray to God to be merciful and kind to those in need. But intercession is more than this. The word in Latin means to take a step which puts us at the heart of a situation, like a man who stands between two people about to fight.[2]

Just as we must never forget the spiritual reality of our place before the throne of God, so must we also remember that we are in a spiritual battle. When Christ died on the cross to pay the price for our sins the battle was won. Thanks be to God through our Lord Jesus Christ!

But the skirmishes still go on, and our prayers and ministry are still needed. We join the victorious army when we take on this ministry. As we pray for others while doing healing of the generations, we gather up those we are praying for and storm the gates of heaven until their days of bondage are over!

Trust in Jesus!

Let us then with confidence draw near to the throne of grace, that we may receive mercy and find grace to help in time of need.

Hebrews 4:16

A faithful person in the present generation going before God in strong intercessory prayer can release an entire family from the effects of past generational hurt and sin. As we do this, Jesus himself intercedes both for us and with us. He is our great High Priest, who is continually before the throne of God, pleading for us. We cannot even hope to engage in this ministry without the complete assurance of His help, because healing of generations requires a very powerful form of intercessory prayer. When we take part in it, we become prayer-warriors, people who are engaged in a very intense battle. Our fight is not with a visible foe, but with the Christian's ancient and defeated enemy, Satan.

St. Peter wrote:

Be sober, be watchful. Your adversary the devil prowls around like a roaring lion, seeking someone to devour. Resist him, firm in your faith, knowing that the same experience of suffering is required of Christians throughout the world.

1 Peter 5:8-9 (NRSV)

Our families have been kept in bondage to their hurt and pain for many generations because of the work of this adversary. We are now on the front lines, working with Jesus, in the battle to free all of the members of our families, whether past, present, or future, as Christ restores, establishes, and strengthens us.

In the book *The Hour That Changes the World*, Dick Eastman writes:

...intercession is God's method for involving His followers more completely in the totality of His plan. When we intercede for others we stand at God's side, working together with Him, in the task of redeeming others . . . we have authority to take from the enemy everything he is holding back. The chief way of taking is by prayer, and by whatever action prayer leads us to."[3]

We cannot do this on our own! Empowered by the Holy Spirit, we work in tandem with Jesus. He is always by our side, interceding for us and with us. As Eastman says, Christians have authority through the Name of Jesus to take back anything that Satan is keeping from them. In Jesus' Name we have authority to take our families back by releasing them from the effects of generational sin. In this way we will gain freedom from the enemy's harassment. Thanks be to God for His redeeming love!

Chapter Six

Steps to Healing of Generations

Step 1: Put on the Whole Armor of God

Finally, be strong in the Lord and in the strength of His might. Put on the whole armor of God, so that you may be able to stand against the wiles of the devil. For we are not contending against flesh and blood, but against the principalities, against the powers, against the world rulers of this present darkness, against the spiritual hosts of wickedness in the heavenly places.

Ephesians 6:10-12

Every session of generational healing should begin with special prayers for protection, asking the Holy Spirit to put an invisible shield of security around each person involved - the prayer-counselors, the supplicant, and the family of each one of them. Spiritual protection is available to each Christian, but we have the responsibility of putting it on each day.

Prayer-counselors are extremely vulnerable to harassment by demonic forces. Before I began to use these prayers I would wake up in the middle of the night and feel the strong force of an evil presence in my room. As soon as I called on the Name of Jesus the presence would leave, but the experience left me feeling very vulnerable and disturbed.

Friends suggested I 'put on the whole armor of God', following the directions in Ephesians 6.10ff, and pray the binding prayer that had been gathering dust on my desk. This seemed superstitious to me. I felt that since I was a child of God, baptized into Jesus and covered by His blood, I didn't need any extra protection.

I hadn't taken into account the fact that one who carries on a ministry such as this is in the midst of a battleground and needs to take extra precautions. I went on suffering from this nighttime harassment and others during the daytime. After a while the pressure was too much for me. I began to use the prayers for protection out of desperation and, lo and behold, they worked!

The evil presence never bothered me again, *unless* I forgot to put on my armor! So 'put on the whole armor of God', and pray the prayer of protection the first thing each day and before each prayer session. Here is the prayer of protection given to me by Francis McNutt at a Fishnet Northeast Conference a few years ago:

> In the Name of Jesus Christ and by the power of His cross and blood I bind all of the spirits, powers, and forces of the earth, the air, the water, the fire, the netherworld, the satanic forces of nature, and all satanic and demonic spirits. I break and send to Jesus any curses, contracts, covenants, hexes, spells, or pacts. I bind any demonic interaction, interplay, or communication. I claim the protection of the shed Blood of Jesus over _____ (put in your own name and the names of your loved ones and those whom you are praying with).
>
> If a threatening presence is felt, ask Jesus to send St. Michael the archangel and his army of angels to protect you and drive Satan away. Before going to sleep, commit yourself and your loved ones into Jesus' care and ask Jesus to send His angels to stand guard and protect you and all of your loved ones.

Complete your protection by putting on your spiritual armor daily:

> Therefore take the whole armor of God, that you may be able to withstand in the evil day, and having done all, to stand. Stand therefore, having girded your loins with truth, and having put on the breastplate of righteousness, and having shod your feet with the equipment of the gospel of peace; besides all these, taking the shield of faith, with which you can quench all the flaming darts of the evil one. And take the

helmet of salvation, and the sword of the Spirit, which is the word of God. Pray at all times in the Spirit, with all prayer and supplication. To that end keep alert with all perseverance, making supplication for all the saints . . .

Ephesians 6:13-18

Put on your armor as soon as you wake up each morning, and make sure you don't give into any temptation to take it off throughout the day. Remember, it isn't magic, we have our part to do! Satan loves to tempt us into letting go of our protection.

If we don't trust in Jesus as our Savior and Redeemer, then we step outside of the protection of the helmet of salvation. If we become self-righteous, instead of depending on the righteousness that only Jesus can give us, how can we be shielded by the breastplate of righteousness? If we don't have a strong belief in the promises put forth in Scripture, then how can we be kept safe from the 'fiery darts of the evil one' by the 'shield of faith'?

Only a person who has made and kept a decision to 'speak the truth' can be sure he or she is surrounded by the girdle of truth. If we give in to the easy lie, we can be sure we have stepped out of the protection of our battle gear. We need to quickly go to Jesus in repentance when this happens.

Step 2: Center on Jesus and Follow His Lead!

Jesus said to them, "Truly, truly, I say to you, the Son can do nothing of his own accord, but only what he sees the Father doing; for whatever he does, that the Son does likewise. For the Father loves the Son, and shows him all that he himself is doing; and greater works than these will he show you, that you may marvel."

John 5:19-20

In these verses Jesus sets an example for all of us who would follow in His footsteps. As He was sent to this earth to do His Father's work and so does 'only what He sees the Father doing', so we, when we are praying for the healing of generations, must do only what we see the Son doing. We center on Jesus. He is the Healer. He leads us, step-by-step, through the time of prayer.

So, as we are praying through the generations of a person's family, we keep our eyes on Jesus and do only what we see Him doing. We do not depend on our own skills, or on what we do or do not know. We depend completely on the leading of the Holy Spirit, who gives us the discernment and understanding we need. We depend on Jesus and His desire to heal His people.

We begin by trusting not in our own faith and ability, but in Jesus' love and faithfulness. Before we begin to pray, we take the time to sit quietly in Jesus' presence, until we feel Him with us. We pray quietly in the Spirit, praising Jesus and thanking Him for the healing He is going to bring into the supplicant's life. Then we wait until we feel the Holy Spirit leading us, before starting prayer for the generations of the supplicant's family.

As we go into prayer, we usually have no idea how we are to proceed. The Holy Spirit will lead us by a thought that comes unbidden into our minds, or by a strong inner feeling that we are to proceed in a certain way. At times we feel the need to ask the supplicant more questions to clarify the situation. At other times one or more of us may begin to see a picture of something that happened in the past.

Sometimes the most difficult thing is to learn to trust what we are receiving. However, when we are able to trust the leading we receive from Jesus and share it with the others who are praying with us, they will usually confirm it in some way. Then it will become clearer as we proceed to describe it to one another.

"Again I say to you, if two of you agree on earth about anything they ask, it will be done for them by my Father in heaven. For where two or three are gathered in my name, there am I in the midst of them."

Matthew 18:19-20

As Jesus states in these verses, when we call for His help He will always be there for us. He never fails us. He is always delighted to bring those we intercede for into total healing. It is we who must learn to trust in His never-failing love and healing power.

We don't really know where we're going in any particular healing session, how we'll get there, or what we'll have to do along the way. A common feeling is, "This is the one case that we won't know how to handle." But this isn't true, it's only our old enemy trying to get us to give up on the person with us. *There are no incurable cases in healing of generations!* As long as people are willing to go through the hard work required, they and their family members will be healed!

As we lean totally on Jesus for guidance, admitting our own helplessness, He shows Himself trustworthy by shining His light of love into every dark and difficult situation we come upon. The truth is, we don't know how to bring anyone to healing, but Jesus does. That's all that is important!

When we don't know what to do, we ask Jesus to show us. When we don't understand what is happening, or where the hurt has come from, we ask Jesus to explain. He will direct us, He will give us the wisdom and understanding that we need. We will know that it is He who is doing the healing, and not we, ourselves. We rely totally on the inspiration Jesus gives us through the guidance of the Holy Spirit. He gives us the gifts of wisdom, knowledge, and discernment. Through visions, words of knowledge, and inner feelings, He reveals at each moment how we are to proceed with each individual problem that presents itself.

An example of this was the case of a woman we will call Janice who came to me because her husband had never really accepted their third daughter. He wanted very much to have a son. He didn't mind having the first two daughters, but when the third came he didn't want anything to do with her.

Janice and I went into prayer, asking Jesus to tell us why this was so. Suddenly, Janice said, "This can't be happening!" She was seeing something that seemed very strange to her. She described the vision she was getting of an elderly Italian man on the deck of a vessel that was heading for Ellis Island. She said again, "This can't be happening, I've never been there." I told her to relax and continue to tell me what she was seeing. The picture becomes much clearer as you describe it to someone else, because as you describe it you must look at it more closely yourself.

Then Janice told me the elderly man was getting on a bus. By this time I could see the picture, too. I suggested she ask Jesus to show her where he was going. She said again, "This can't be happening! He's going to Ohio, and I've never known anyone from Ohio." I told her to stick with the picture Jesus was giving her and He would make sense out of it.

Then Janice said again, "This can't be happening!" The man had gotten off of the bus in Ohio, and found no one there to meet him. Officials had then found out that his son had left Ohio to live in Rhode Island.

Then I asked what the man was doing about this. She said he had gotten on a bus headed for Rhode Island. I asked if she could see Jesus with him. She said no. I felt strongly that Jesus was on the bus, too. Then she said again, "This can't be happening! Jesus is driving the bus!" And, indeed, there was Jesus in the driver's seat, enjoying Himself immensely.

The bus eventually drove into Providence. When the man got off of it, his son was there waiting for him. I then suggested Janice ask Jesus what all of this had to do with her husband. Jesus led us to understand that the son was her husband's father. The next scene He showed us was of the son working on the father's farm and taking care of him in his old age. Then we heard the father say, "Everyone has to have a son to take care of him in his old age." This feeling had come down in the family line and was behind her husband's rejection of his third daughter.

If you study this episode, you can see how the Holy Spirit informed us and led us from one part of it to another through pictures He put into our minds, through inner feelings, and through words of knowledge. It is important to remember that as Jesus shows us scenes from our family's past, we just relax and let Him take over.

Jesus is the Healer and He only brings hurts up into our consciousness because they need healing and He intends to heal them! He brings us to the place where we can go back into the pain of a dysfunctional family system in order to have it healed. He knows why the people in our family reacted to life in the way that they did. He alone knows how to take the rocks and brambles and weeds out of our lives in such a way that the wounds left by them are completely healed.

Step 3: A Time of Prayer

Consequently he is able for all time to save those who draw near to God through him, since he always lives to make intercession for them. Hebrews 7:25

Healing of generations is done in much the same way as healing of memories. We begin in a prayerful attitude, centering in on Jesus. We acknowledge His presence with us, and His acute desire to heal the person we are praying with. We ask Him to give us a spirit of discernment and of knowledge, so that in each situation that presents itself we will understand His will.

We watch Jesus and listen to Him, as He leads us and brings His healing love to bear on every situation that we encounter. If we don't understand what is going on, we question Him, "Why did this happen?", or, "Show us how you intend to bring this into healing," or, "What do you want us to do about this?" All through the time of prayer we keep our minds and hearts attuned to Jesus.

When Jesus shows a hurting moment from the past, ask Him to go into it. Let Him take over the action. Always turn the supplicant back to Jesus, especially if he or she is worried. Direct attention to Him: "What is Jesus doing?" "Go to Jesus," if the supplicant is frightened. "Ask Jesus," if he or she wonders why someone is hurting a member of the family line. Only Jesus can show such overwhelming love that it heals even the greatest hurt. Only He can answer the question of why our ancestors behaved the way they did.

We have found that our prayer is more effective when we work in teams of two. Therefore, at each healing session we have three people: two prayer partners and the person who wishes healing, or the supplicant. This gives us more security in case we experience any difficulties, such as a need for deliverance.

One of the reasons I always have a prayer partner with me when praying for healing of the generations is to receive more insight into what approach we are to follow in prayer. The second reason is that when two or more people receive the same leading it gives the confirmation we need in order to be sure we are indeed following the Lord's lead. This comes as each one of us shares the visions, words of knowledge, and inner feelings that come as we engage in prayer, and find that they all add up to one whole pattern of discernment.

Three people working together also assures us that there will be more spiritual power and more spiritual gifts at hand. Each one of the three will receive some leading from the Holy Spirit. One person may be able to see the action taking place, while another receives a word of knowledge that tells us how to pray, and the other may simply have a strong inner feeling that we are to proceed in a certain way. In this way the Lord gives us the confirmation that assures us we are truly following His lead.

Step 4: The Genogram: A Tool for Healing

We begin to do healing of the generations by first making up a generational chart, or genogram, to show us what the family's problems are. A genogram is a very useful tool that has long been used by people working with a family systems approach to counseling. By glancing at the genogram I can see each generation with its particular problems arrayed clearly. I can see where problems began and also back check during the prayer time to make sure each problem has been covered. This is a tool the Holy Spirit uses to show me where the greatest prayer is needed.

I have each supplicant make up a genogram that goes back three or four generations. Very few people know anything about their family history past their great-grandparents, so to include any more in the genogram would be a waste of time. If we need to go any further back into the generations of a person's family line, Jesus will show us as we begin praying for them.

First, we document the problems coming down through the family tree vertically and then horizontally. By vertically, I mean those problems that are passed down from one generation to another, as from grandfather to father to son. By horizontally, I mean those that are going from one person to another in one generation, as from sibling to sibling, or from cousin to cousin.

Then I look at the genogram to see the patterns of pain, ill health, addictions, or abusive behavior that are coming down through the family line. I then pray over it to get a feeling of what Jesus wants to heal first. There may be many problems in a person's family line that need healing, but only Jesus knows which one we need to address first. So I rely on the inner visions and feelings He gives me. I sometimes call these feelings my 'nudgies', because I feel that I am being nudged by Jesus to go in a certain direction. This is just a strong inner feeling to proceed in a certain manner.

As each episode of prayer is finished, we check the genogram again to see just what has been healed and what still needs prayer. As we do this, Jesus will enlighten our minds so that we will understand just how this particular healing interconnects with the rest of the family's problems. As we look at the genogram, He will give us the discernment to know just what hurts we need to pray for next. Remember, we don't stop praying until we have reached the root cause of each hurt. (An example of a genogram is in Appendix A.)

Step 5: The Holy Eucharist: Breaking up Logjams

Before going into prayer for generational healing with a supplicant, I first pray a prayer of protection for the supplicant (the person who has come for healing of generations), my prayer partner, myself, and all of our loved ones. This is to protect us from any onslaught of the evil forces which may have held the supplicant's family in bondage for many generations.

We then celebrate the Holy Eucharist with the specific intention of cutting off any pain, sin, spiritual, or emotional bondage that is coming down through the generations of that person's family line. This bondage may come from great sins that were committed by the supplicant's forebears, or by great hurts that were perpetrated by someone else against the supplicant's forebears.

I can compare this to the breaking up of a logjam in a river. In order to break the logjam, which is keeping the river from flowing smoothly to its destination, you have to find the large log around which all of the debris is clustered. As soon as this log is removed, the small branches and leaves that were caught around it are released, and the water rushes freely down stream once again. As we celebrate the Holy Eucharist for the generational lines of a family, the Lord takes us to the logjam back in the family's past history that is the source of the greatest problems in that family line. This is almost always a great sin that has been committed by someone, or against someone, in the past generations of the family line.

Anne's story is an example of a logjam that was effectively removed, freeing many generations of people, but, in particular, Anne and her mother. Anne came to me because she had been so badly hurt by her mother as she was growing up. Her mother was a self-centered woman who never thought of anyone but herself. Anne hated to go to see her mother because she never talked of anything but her own complaints. She came to me because she was expecting her mother for a visit and could not bear the thought of being with her for several days.

After celebrating the Eucharist for the breaking of bondage in Anne's family line, we asked the Lord to show us what had happened back in the generations of her mother's family that had resulted in her mother having such bitterness and self-absorption. In prayer we found that an ancestor involved in witchcraft had caused the problems that came down through her family line.

This is what Anne experienced during prayers for generational healing:

The Lord took me to the patio of our house. I was about seven or eight years old. It was the end of a scene in which my mother had been particularly hateful and mean to me. I asked the Lord why my mother was so hateful to me. Suddenly, she came out onto the patio and became a girl standing in front of her mother, with her head down, being shamed.

Then I saw a whole line of women, going back many generations, in shame and darkness. After that I saw an ugly, warty witch with a huge nose and green skin, in a coven around a cauldron. I asked Jesus to be there and, as I did this, He came and immediately commanded the demon in her to come out. Then I asked Him to forgive her, and I sent my forgiveness back through the generations to this woman. Immediately, the woman's black robes fell off. She had on a lovely white dress with blue flowers. Her hair turned light. It was braided and wrapped around her head. She rebuked the evil spirits in the rest of her coven, and they all were gone.

Then children sprang up like flowers around her and began dancing. She turned out to be a gentle, kind woman. She was now in a bright, flower-filled meadow. She began throwing flowers, and the light of Christ, onto all of the succeeding generations of women. As she did this, they became light and happy, including my mother and my grandmother. My mother and my grandmother especially felt happy together. Then my little girl mother played with little girl me. We danced and put on a "show" (which I did at that age for the neighborhood) together. It felt good to play with my mother. She was fun!

This occurred about a week before my mother came for a visit. In the past she has driven me crazy and completely drained me by the time she left, but this turned out to be one of the best visits we've ever had. So good, in fact, that I was able to do some inner healing prayer with her, which was very healing for both of us. I continue to see wonderful changes in my mother. Her self-centeredness is gone and I enjoy spending time with her.

The logjam back in the generations of Anne's family line happened to be the woman who was engaging in witchcraft. When we celebrated the Eucharist for the generations of her family, the sin of witchcraft was cut off and its effect on the family line made null and void. Thus the logjam was broken and the way clear to bring Jesus' love and healing power to bear on the hurts she and her mother had received.

Although it may be difficult to find a clergy person who will celebrate a Eucharist for the generations of your family line, it is well worth the effort it would take. The power of the Holy Eucharist to break the back of sin and to bring healing to families and individuals is unsurpassed.

It is most helpful if the Eucharist is offered expressly for the healing of the generational lines of the person you are working with before going into prayer, especially if there are many problems seen on the genogram. If this is not possible, do as much healing as you can for the supplicant's family line, and then have the supplicant take the family chart to a regularly scheduled Eucharist and offer it to the Lord for healing of the bondage coming from the past.

Step 6: Watching the Drama Unfold

As you can see from this case history, as we continue in an attitude of prayer, Jesus brings into our minds a scene from the past generations of the family we are praying for. Usually all of those praying together will see the same scene, or some aspect of it, or they will receive some inner knowledge, or discernment, about it. It is in this way that the Lord confirms that this vision is truly from Him.

As Jesus shows the hurting situation to us, we see it being acted out in our mind's eye. The experience is akin to what happens when you are watching a play being acted out upon a stage, only there is much more urgency to it. When you first begin to watch a play, you are very aware that you are separated from the action. However, as you become more interested in it, you also become more intensely involved, until you feel as if you were actually taking part in the drama yourself. This is the way it is during prayer for the healing of generations.

You actually feel as if you were there, reliving an event that is making a very dramatic impact on your life. You feel the emotions of your ancestors and those interacting with them as you watch the incident being replayed in your mind. It is at this point that you ask Jesus into the scene to bring His healing love to bear upon the people and events you see in it.

Most people will immediately see Jesus in the scene with them. Some only sense His presence, or see a bright light. Other people, who may be deeply hurting or have a great many problems back in the generations, may not be able to see Him at all without a lot of help.

I usually advise people to take their time, pray quietly for a while, and then look around for Jesus. Sometimes He is at the outer fringes of the picture, waiting to be asked to come closer. Some people are not at all visual. They may never see anything, but as the prayer-counselors see a hurting situation from their past and pray for Jesus to heal it, they will still experience the deep love of Jesus flowing through it and be healed just as a more visual person would.

In the beginning of each session, we take a lot of time to focus on Jesus and, while praying softly in the Spirit, we wait for a scene to develop in the supplicant's mind. Sometimes it is important to do some healing of hurting childhood memories before we can go to the hurts of past generations. At other times we have to clean out a lot of debris from the past before the supplicant's childhood hurts can be healed.

Step 7: Do Whatever He Tells You

These words that Mary, Jesus' mother, uttered at the wedding in Cana inform our actions during a healing episode; we are to do whatever Jesus tells us to. We can never predict what Jesus will do. He is extremely creative and His action will depend on what caused the hurt in the first place. We wait upon Him in an attitude of prayer and He brings into our mind's eye pictures of the things that have happened in our family's past that need to be redeemed by him. We say a simple prayer, "Jesus, please show us what you want to heal in the generations of this family."

Then we wait until He brings a hurting situation into our minds. He may start with some abusive situation that the supplicant remembers from his or her childhood and then take us back one or more generations to similar situations in his or her parents' or grandparents' lives. Each time Jesus shows us a hurting situation, we ask Him to go into it and bring it into healing. After He has healed one episode, we ask Him to take us back further to the root cause, the origin of the hurt, and bring it into healing, also.

We always know when we have reached the root cause by the sense of finality and peace we receive. It's a feeling of "Yes. This is finally it. We have arrived at the original hurt or sin and it has been healed!" At each step along the way we ask Jesus into the episode He is showing us to bring healing to it.

In healing of generations we depend completely on Jesus, and He never lets us down! This is His ministry. He will lead us from beginning to end. He brings a situation from out of the past into our mind's eye. As soon as we see it, we ask Him to come into it to heal it. Then we not only watch Him, but we also listen to Him.

He will give us the discernment that will let us know what to do in each situation, and He will give us the understanding we need so that we will know why this situation hurt the family. He will tell us how the trauma can be healed. We know from experience that He will stop anything in the scene He shows us that is hurtful and He will comfort those who have been abused.

Step 8: Expressing Emotions

Be angry but do not sin; do not let the sun go down on your anger . . .

Ephesians 4:26

As we go through healing of generations, we often see events happening that caused great pain to people in the past generations of our family. Very often their pain has come down through the family line to us, and as we see the hurt that was done to them we also feel the anger and frustration that they originally felt. It is normal to be angry when someone hurts you. However, as these verses from the Epistle to the Ephesians tell us, we must be careful what we do with our anger: "...do not sin; do not let the sun go down on your anger."

It is not good to hold on to our anger and let it roil up within us until it becomes resentment and bitterness. Anger that is held onto leads to bitterness that begins to work like poison within a person. It is the same with any other negative emotion we experience. Whether anger, fear, despair, or shame; any negative emotion can take on a life of its own, like a cancer that spreads throughout one's whole system. It causes untold spiritual, physical, and emotional damage to the persons holding it, their families, and the generations of people coming after them down through the family lines.

So, as soon as Jesus has brought healing into the situation we are praying for, we should work through any hurtful emotions we are feeling. We do this by expressing our feelings to the people responsible for hurting our family. While we are still in prayer for the healing of a particular situation back in the generations, we express the emotions we are feeling to the person who hurt our ancestors. When we do this, we are standing in for every member of our family line, whether living or dead.

Sometimes it is someone from our family line who has caused great pain to come down through the generations and affect our lives. Sometimes it is someone outside the family who has caused this. Whoever it is, while Jesus is still present in the memory with us, we should express our feelings to the person who caused the hurt.

It doesn't matter how long ago this happened. The wounds coming down through the family line are still raw and open until the anger arising from them has been expressed and they have been healed and laid to rest. So the person who is experiencing the healing, while still seeing the inner vision, tells those in the vision who are responsible for the pain how this has made them feel.

Thus, if I were the one hurt, I would see myself in the vision, interacting with those who hurt my family and I would say something like this: "You shouldn't have done that, you hurt my family very much. I am very angry at you." I might sob and rage, I might shout out my anger, or I might be very quiet about it. However I did this, the important thing is to get in touch with my genuine inner feelings and express them.

Sometimes as the supplicants express their emotions, it is as though I see Jesus standing in front of them pulling dirty rags out of their mouths. These dirty rags are indicative of the poison coming from the resentment and unforgiveness that have been in their family lines for generations. As we speak out our feelings of hurt, the rawness of our inner wounds begins to fade, because we feel Jesus' love filling and healing all of our individual hurts *and* the generational hurts that caused them. The knowledge He gives us of why the hurt occurred also pours soothing balm on our wounds.

After our pain has been healed, and the emotions coming from them expressed, the next step is for the supplicants to forgive those who have hurt them.

Step 9: The Importance of Forgiveness

Truly, I say to you, whatever you bind on earth shall be bound in heaven, and whatever you loose on earth shall be loosed in heaven.

Matthew 18:18

After Jesus has healed the situation, and the supplicant has expressed his or her emotional reaction to it, it is necessary to go through a process of forgiveness in order for the healing to be totally effective. Here the supplicant is standing in for all of the members of the family, living and dead.

Jesus will lead us in this. He will give us discernment as to just what needs to be done in each individual case. This is a three-step process. The supplicant begins by asking Jesus to forgive the person or persons who caused the pain and hurt to come into the family line. The supplicant then extends forgiveness to the perpetrators on behalf of the other members of the family line, thereby breaking off any bondage that might be coming down through the generations because of this problem. Then the supplicant asks Jesus for forgiveness for anyway in which he or she has engaged in the same type of sin.

That is, if a spirit of revenge came down in the family line because of some great hurt that was done to the family in past generations, and the supplicant has also harbored vengeful feelings, he or she needs to ask Jesus for forgiveness before the hurt will be totally healed.

Usually, our Lord puts it on our hearts to continue to intercede for the sinful members of past generations until we see them go to Him in submission, and feel that He has forgiven them. We often see their clothing, or something about them, change from dark to light as they kneel in front of Him as if asking forgiveness.

At other times we may simply feel a great burden that is lifted as we pray for their forgiveness. As this happens, we ask Jesus to put His cross and His blood, the symbols of His authority and His power, between these people and the rest of the family line. When He has done this, the effects of their sin will no longer hurt this family in any way.

Let me emphasize, in order for this reconciliation to be complete it is necessary for the supplicant, as a representative of the family being healed, to extend forgiveness to the ancestor. The family as a whole has been deeply hurt by the actions of this ancestor. This hurt needs to be acknowledged and the problem worked through to forgiveness, if the family line is to receive true healing and release from the bondage that their ancestor's sin has put them in.

In Matthew 18:18 Jesus says:

> whatever you bind on earth shall be bound in heaven, and whatever you loose on earth shall be loosed in heaven.

We are in the business of binding and loosing all of the time. By our reaction to each thing that is done to us, we either bind or let loose those around us. If we forgive those who hurt us we let them loose, whether they are in this world or the next. We bind them and keep them bound as long as we fail to forgive them. Indeed, forgiveness may be the most important ingredient in bringing complete healing to our family line. When we are praying through a generational line, we sometimes see chains, coming from centuries of bondage, falling away from those we are in the process of forgiving.

When this happens, we are joining with Jesus in His work as Redeemer. We are standing with Him as He hung on the cross and said, "Father, forgive them, for they do not know what they are doing." We are one with Him as He compassionately forgives those who caused His death, even as He was still dying on the cross. If we ask Him, He will give us the understanding and unconditional love we need in order to have mercy on those who have sinned against our families.

When we don't forgive those who have hurt us, we are really saying to God, "I am going to hold these people captive with my anger until they have made complete restoration to me." We seem to feel that forgiving a person is the same thing as condoning the wrong they have done.

It is not the same! To forgive as an act of our will never means to condone hurtful or sinful actions. To forgive is to take an action that will give that person over into God's hands and begin a process that will unbind both the perpetrator and the victim from the consequences of the wrong that has been done. It is saying to Jesus, "Your will be done. I will allow you your rightful place as Judge of the living and the dead. I will trust that you know what is best for this person, for myself, and for the rest of my family."

> Behold, never avenge yourself, but leave it to the wrath of God, for it is written, vengeance is mine, I will repay, says the Lord . . . Do not be overcome by evil, but overcome evil with good.
>
> Romans 12:19,21

It is the wounds from unforgiveness and bitterness that continue to plague our families for generation after generation. Sometimes we find that we ourselves have hurt the family by the way that we have reacted to the problems that have been passed on to us. We may have acted out the family's hurt in our own lives by also engaging in some kind of dysfunctional behavior. In some situations it almost seems as though a predisposition to sin in the same way the ancestors did has come down through the generations. In a case like this, it is important for the supplicant to acknowledge any way in which he or she has given in to this temptation, and to ask God for forgiveness for it. This needs to be done so that the bondage that has come down through the generations from that particular sin can be completely broken. So, at this point, we turn to Jesus and ask His forgiveness for the ways in which we have done this. He is always quick to forgive. There are times when the strongest emotion a person feels is anger at God. This is common for people who have been hurt, especially if their ancestors were the victims of someone else's sinful action. The person then needs to know that it is okay to be angry with God, and to express that anger in the same way anger toward any other individual would be expressed. They also may need some help to correct their image of God, so that they will be able to feel comfortable with the understanding that it was not God who caused the hurt to the family.

Step 10: Understanding A Holy God

For I am the Lord your God; consecrate yourselves therefore, and be holy, for I am holy.

Leviticus 11:44

Sometimes we all need a refresher course teaching us more about the character and actions of our heavenly Father. God is holy! God is just and merciful! God is love! It is totally inconsistent with His character to do anything to hurt a person or a family. But God has given us free will, and He will not go against that. In each hurting situation, someone's free will has shut Him out so that He cannot protect His people from harm. We cannot hold Him responsible for what some other person has done! God desires our complete healing. He only asks that we turn back to Him in repentance and love, then He will bring us and all of the members of our family into complete healing.

In the above verses from Leviticus, God is telling us that we are to love, serve and obey only Him. In this there is both joy and safety. It is as though God had called us to Him and put His arms around us in love and protection. This is where He wants us to stay, so that we can be safe from any harm. The only thing that could take us out of this circle of protection is our own willful action.

The Lord God gave us free will. When we use that free will to turn away from Him, He allows us to do that. But in so doing we reap the consequences of our own behavior and lose the protection of His covenantal embrace. Outside of that protection we find many things that can bring harm to us. *But it is not God who is causing the harm.*

The people who have turned away from God to some form of idolatry have removed themselves from God's protection, and are actually bringing upon themselves the logical consequences of their own wayward behavior. *Therefore, I, by my own behavior, can cause either curse or blessing to come to my progeny.*

In *How to Walk with God,* Everett Fullam states,

> The most distinguishable characteristic of the God of Abraham, Isaac, and Jacob, the God and Father of our Lord Jesus Christ, is His holiness. It's not His great power. It's not His infinite wisdom or knowledge. It's His holy character, with no dark spots, no shadows, rather light through and through.
>
> His holiness means a consistency of purpose that is never deflected and a constancy of devotion in continual and eternal covenant. If we are going to be among those who seek the Lord, we must concern ourselves with His holiness - and concentrate on responding with a personal holiness that conforms to the will and purpose of God.[1]

Yes, God calls us into a holy walk with Him, and when people go to Him in love and commitment, asking Him to bring healing to their families, He answers their plea with a hearty "Yes!" The good news is, that in spite of our wayward, willful actions, *God never gives up on us.* In His deep faithfulness, God calls us to Him and showers us with His unconditional, overflowing love.

As Deuteronomy 20:10 affirms, when a person turns back to God in love and obedience, He showers upon that person His steadfast love. Within that love is contained a promise of complete healing for that person and all of the generations of that person's family through the ministry of our Lord Jesus Christ.

Step 11: Cleansing Prayer

If any think they are religious, and do not bridle their tongues but deceive their hearts, their religion is worthless.

James 1:26 (NRSV)

After we have finished one episode of generational prayer, we check the genogram again to see what else in the family lines needs healing. We continue to ask Jesus to show us the root cause of the family's hurt until we are satisfied that everything is healed. We will know it is healed if the supplicant now feels filled with the peace of Jesus. However, it may take a series of prayer sessions before every problem has been prayed through.

When the time of ministry is over the prayer-counselors still have work to do. We must cleanse ourselves of any hurt, emotional garbage, or demonic attachment we may have picked up during the time of prayer. Even though we have prayed the prayers of protection, evil spirits may still try to cling to us after a healing session. These can be easily removed by a prayer of cleansing.

After each time of prayer-counseling I picture Jesus bringing us to a beautiful waterfall at the edge of some woods and washing us clean as we stand under it. As Jesus washes us, we pray a binding prayer, telling Satan and all of his minions to leave us and go to the place He has prepared for them, asking for further protection for ourselves and our families, and for safe travel home. At this time we also give into Jesus' care everything we have heard and seen during the healing session. We give to Him our tongues and our minds, so that we will not be tempted to repeat or ruminate over any part of the supplicant's history or healing. This is of utmost importance! People entrust their most personal thoughts and feelings to us. This is a sacred trust, and we must not violate it in any way!

We then pray to be refilled with the Spirit's energizing power. When this is done, we feel refreshed, cleansed, and renewed by our Lord's ministry to us.

Here are some further suggestions to help you maintain confidentiality:

♦   Before each session of prayer ask Jesus to let everything you hear and see go immediately to Him, so that you are only a channel of His continued blessing for this person, not a repository for his or her hurts.

♦   After each session ask the Holy Spirit to put a seal upon your mind, heart, and lips, so that you will never even think of repeating anything from the session.

♦   If you are ever tempted to reveal anything heard in the time of prayer realize Jesus is always close at hand to help, all you need do is ask.   If you continue to have this temptation stop ministering and go to your priest, pastor, or a counselor for help.

♦   *Always* ask the supplicant's permission if you feel the need to discuss his or her problems with another person.

♦   If you feel overwhelmed by the problems of the person you are praying for, refer him or her to another prayer-counselor or to a psychotherapist.

♦   Remember to continue to seek help for your own emotional and spiritual needs. Take time off to play and enjoy yourself.

As with anything else in this ministry, protection and confidentiality come only as we give ourselves and our ministry to our Lord Jesus Christ. We will be kept in perfect peace as we keep *everything* in our lives focused on Him.

A very important ingredient in the healing process is the Body of Christ. Both the people who are in the process of having Jesus heal great hurts, and the prayer-counselors helping them, need to receive the sacraments regularly for strength and healing. They need to study Scripture and get their lives in line with Biblical principles. They need the understanding support of the clergy and the prayerful and loving help of other Christians.

Healing is a process. It begins when people desire wholeness so much that they are willing to go into the great pain that is coming down through their family lines in order to receive it. It continues to take effect as they work to let go of anger and bitterness and become ready to forgive those who hurt them and the members of their families.

It goes on as they put aside bad habits and thought patterns and replace them with Christian ways of thinking and living. The process is completed as they become willing to stand up and take charge of their own lives, always leaning on the love of Christ, the power of the Holy Spirit, and the fellowship of other Christians to enable them in this journey toward wholeness.

Step 12: A Grateful Heart and Mind

Not only with our ancestors did the Lord make this covenant, but with us, who are all of us here alive today.

Deuteronomy 5:3

The most common feeling at the end of a session of healing of generations is one of humility and gratitude. We know that it was not our great knowledge or our marvelous skill, but Jesus' love and power that brought this person to healing. We go to Him in utter helplessness, and He brings total healing. "Not by might, not by power, but by my spirit, says the Lord" (Zechariah 4:6). And we never doubt that is how the healing of the family we have been praying for has come about.

After people have received healing of generations, I advise them to take some time to prayerfully look over their families' past history in order to get in touch with the good things that have come down through the family lines. As this is done they can thank God for the good received from the past generations. Then I suggest that they ask God to send their thanks and love back through the generations to those who will receive them.

I'm very careful to make sure that the supplicant is ready for this step. To suggest it too soon would only lead to more pain for those with deep hurts that are not yet completely healed, such as incest victims. I wait until people have received enough healing to be able to completely forgive those who hurt them before doing this. Then I have them look for the blessings that have come to them from their families.

I mentioned in Chapter 2 that one of the good things that have come down in my family line is the love of gardening. I have been filled with thankfulness so many times because my father was a farmer. I don't even know if I can communicate how deeply I feel about it. I simply love to be on my knees, digging in my garden. Time seems to stand still, and I feel at one with my Creator, as I dig and plant and weed.

To me this is a wonderful gift, and I am eternally grateful for it. I feel as though it has been passed down through the generations of my family just for our joy! I regularly thank my heavenly Father for this gift, and I ask Him to send my thankfulness to my earthly father so that he can know the pleasure it has given to me and to my children. I think it must be a source of blessing to my dad to know that he has left such a beautiful legacy to his children. I also feel blessed because our sons seem to love gardening as much as I do, I hope that this will be a gift that they pass on to their children.

My mother gave a wonderful gift of cooking to her family. This is how she showed her love to all of us. She loved to cook, and no matter what she cooked, it was delicious! Our sons seem to have inherited this gift, too. Each one is an excellent cook, and each married a woman who is also a gifted cook. I can't wait to see how our grandchildren carry on this heritage!

Mom also had a wonderful gift of hospitality and would invite the whole family to a picnic on a moment's notice. Not a small event when you realize that she had eleven children, thirty-nine grandchildren, and who-knows-how-many great-grandchildren, and we had any number of assorted cousins, aunts, uncles, nieces, and nephews, all of whom would come over at the drop of a hat! These gatherings were a source of much joy to me and my family.

I continually ask God to send my thanks back to my mother as a blessing for this gift and any others that she gave me. I also ask Him regularly to thank my parents for the gift of life and love that they gave to me. So often we forget that our very presence in this life is a gift that our parents gave to us.

I am very grateful to God for healing the hurts that have come down in my own family lines. Because of this healing, I have been freed to serve Him and offer His healing love to others. It is because I have been healed that I really desire with all my heart to see others healed. This desire reaches back through all of the generations of my family tree to those who would receive it, as I send my love to those in past generations of my father's and mother's family lines, and ask God to also send His blessings upon them, and all of their progeny, too.

Chapter Seven

Testimonies to Generational Healing

Celeste

Blessed be the Lord,
   for he has heard the voice of my supplications.
The Lord is my strength and my shield;
   in him my heart trusts;
so I am helped, and my heart exults,
   and with my song I give thanks to him.
                                        Psalm 28:6,7

Celeste came to me when she discovered that she had fibroid tumors. She was a black woman who came from a line of women who, in every generation, had serious problems with their reproductive systems. In the healing of generations we asked Jesus to show us what had caused this in her family.

As we began to pray, we saw the home of a tribe which appeared to be living on the planes of Africa in beautiful lake country. We saw the leader of this tribe, a very strong and demanding man. He was particularly interested in the birth of boy children to do the work of the tribe.

When girls were born, he would often order them to be drowned. In his anger over the birth of girl children, he would blame the mothers and punish them. Jesus showed us that this produced generational feelings of fear, shame, and guilt over being born female and that the women in her family reacted physically through the manifestation of genito-reproductive diseases.

As Jesus began to heal this condition, we saw Him gather all of the mothers to Him, and He gave them back their daughters. They were beautiful dark-eyed little girls. As Jesus brought healing and unbound the generations from the curse that had resulted from this sin, Celeste felt as though her tumors were healed. Later, when Celeste saw her doctor to find out if any further treatment was needed, the doctor found that the tumors were still there, but had not changed in size. Surprisingly, Celeste has had no symptoms manifested since that time.

Celeste also described a long pattern of rifts between the mothers and first born daughters in her family line. We asked the Lord to reveal the source of this rift. Jesus again took us back to Africa and showed us a sister and a brother playing around the reed-filled waters of an African lake. The little boy fell into the water and drowned. The little girl tried in vain to save him. When the little girl was not able to save him, her mother blamed her for the death of her brother. Because of this incident a bondage of anger and blame held all of the women in the family.

When we asked Jesus to heal the situation, He came into the scene and went directly to the little boy. He placed His face near the little boy's face and breathed new life into him. As the boy moved and came alive, Jesus gave the grieving mother back her son. The mother was so overjoyed that she called the entire village to come and meet this marvelous Man who had given her back her son.

The Lord then brought the mother and daughter together. He took the daughter over to the mother and stood with the little girl holding her close by His side. He told the mother that the child was not to blame for the little boy's death. He asked the mother to forgive her daughter for the death of the child and not hold onto to her anger.

He told this mother that she had placed too much pressure on her daughter by expecting her to be totally responsible for her brother. The mother then went to her little girl and told her that she really did love her. The Lord also allowed the little girl to tell her mother how she felt about being blamed for her brother's death. When the mother heard her daughter speak of her feelings of pain and guilt, she asked her forgiveness.

After this healing took place, Celeste revealed that her own daughters would often say to her, "Mom, don't blame me for . . ." Since we prayed, her children haven't said this any more because Celeste has stopped blaming them for things that were not their responsibility.

After we saw these scenes of healing, we could see that the people in the village were very curious about Jesus. He introduced Himself to them. When He did this, the people began to praise Jesus and accept Him as their Lord. As Celeste watched this healing, she began to marvel at what she was hearing. The people began to sing as they accepted Jesus. They were singing a beautiful song she had never heard before!

In another session we were praying about a pattern of deeply hurtful sexual abuse of the female children that seemed to manifest itself in every generation. As we prayed about these problems, the Lord showed us many scenes from the days when the family was held as slaves by plantation owners. Time after time He showed us how sexual sins committed by the owners against that family would beget problems in the family as brothers and fathers saw their wives and sisters and daughters abused by the owners. Jesus, in His mercy, brought forgiveness and healing into each one of these situations. After we had asked Him into all of these scenes, He began to reveal the root cause of many generations of sexual bondage and pain.

We saw that the founder of Celeste's family line had been an African king and that her direct ancestor had been a royal princess and daughter of this king. Jesus showed us that this man had formed a pact with slave traders who would come deep into African territory hunting for people that they would capture and take to America and sell.

To appease the traders he began to sell members of this tribe to them. In order to keep a supply of men and women to sell, he began to force the women in the tribe into sexual relations in order to breed the children for sale. He even forced his own daughter to engage in these activities, so that the rest of the tribe would accept this terrible atrocity.

We asked Jesus to come into this situation to heal the hurts of this woman and of all these people. As He delivered them from all of the sexual bondage that had occurred, we saw Him give peace and healing to all the people and quiet the weeping of the young women.

After He brought peace to those who had been hurt by this terrible practice we saw Him go to the king and confront him. Jesus asked him to repent so that he could be forgiven. Then Celeste saw this very tall man with high cheekbones, wearing a leopard skin on his body and a magnificent plumage on his head, point his spear at the Lord and command Him to bow down to him, as he refused to repent. When he did this, Jesus made a gesture that indicated He was cutting him off from the family line. He then indicated that He was placing His blood and His cross between this king and all of his descendants so that His healing could come into the entire generational line.

In yet another session, we saw a woman traveling to America on a boat. She was carrying an infant in her arms – a small boy. We could see that she followed an ancient custom of her people and placed a spell of protection over the boy as soon as he was born. The spell was to ward off evil spirits and to protect him against the white man. Celeste revealed that often in her family there had been the practice of mixing "old magic," in the form of voodoo, with the Christian faith that had been adopted by her forebears.

We asked Jesus to come into the scene with this young mother. Jesus went to the woman and took the child into His arms. He then gathered the mother to His side and told her that this practice was not of Him. He also told her that He, Jesus, was the child's protector and God, and that the old practices of magic in her family had to be renounced. He invited her to repent and leave the magic and voodoo behind. He asked her to believe in Him as the one way to God. We then saw the woman repent and accept Jesus as her Savior. When she did this, she received His forgiveness.

Jesus then showed us this boy as an adult. He told us that the boy's name was John. In America John had been sold into slavery. We saw John as a man struggling to make sense of the war inside his being. The war was caused by the spell that his mother had unwittingly placed him under. He wanted to believe in God and trust Jesus. Yet the perception of Jesus as the white man's God was too prevalent. Celeste could see that he had become a faithful Christian, although he often wondered how a God who was supposed to be loving could allow the horrors of slavery to continue.

Celeste could see him sitting with his head collapsed into His hands. We asked Jesus if He would come and comfort John. Jesus came into the scene and touched John on the shoulder. Jesus sat down with John and began to teach him the truth about Himself and His love for **all** humankind. Jesus specifically told John that He loves all black people. When He told him this, John began to weep in His arms. He looked at Jesus and accepted Him totally. We saw that John became a pastor of his church.

Jesus revealed more to us in later sessions about the problems that had befallen the women in Celeste's family. He showed us that there had once been a slave woman named Myrah in Celeste's family, and that Myrah had been twisted by scoliosis. She was severely deformed from years of abuse and from carrying the burden of generations of slavery. She felt compelled to hide herself from the laughter and ridicule which befell her because of her deformity.

When we asked Jesus to come and heal Myrah, we could see a whole black community gathered near a river. Celeste could see Jesus standing in the river inviting them to be baptized by Him. He was dressed in snow white garments. As Myrah slowly went down through the middle of the crowd and into the river, people were laughing and making fun of her. As she stepped into the water Jesus, our Baptizer, took her bent and twisted body and plunged her beneath the water. When she came up, she was dressed in white and her back was straight. As she rose out of the water, she declared that "all of her future generations would be free to sing and praise the Lord."

At that moment Celeste could feel a heat come over her that gave warmth to her entire body, as if she too were receiving the healing that was being given to her ancestor through her prayers. As Celeste began to think about the many gifts that this ancestor could have released in her family, she realized that all of the women and men in her family have beautiful voices. Each one has been raised in the church, and they have all learned to sing praises to His name. It was this faith that had brought Celeste to ask for the healing of the many other problems that seemed prevalent in her family line.

As Celeste's healing has continued to unfold, we have seen the end of cycles of incestuous behavior that were carried down through generations of men and women in her generational lines. As we prayed about the abuse that Celeste had suffered at the hands of her stepfather, Jesus showed us that life on the plantations during the horrors of slavery had a devastating effect on the lives of the men and women in her family line.

When we asked the Lord to show us the root cause of this cycle, He showed us a young slave boy being sexually abused by one of his white owners. We know that it is a truth that when a person is sinned against, that person is also tempted to retaliate and sin against another person. As a result of this abuse, the boy began to work out his rage and pain by abusing his sisters. A cycle of incest which involved both boys and girls was born and continued for generations.

We asked Jesus to touch this boy and heal him at the point in his life where he had been abused by the slave owner. Celeste then asked Jesus to forgive the slave owner, and forgave him herself. Then Jesus showed us that there had been a person in each generation who had continued this cycle of abuse, culminating in her stepfather.

In each instance He showed us, we asked Him in to heal the grievous wounds this perversion had left in the family line. When we saw that the incident had been healed, Celeste forgave the perpetrator and asked Jesus to also forgive that person. We then asked Jesus to cut off all of the people in Celeste's family line from this terrible chain of incest and abuse. Celeste was then able to forgive her stepfather.

There had also been a recurring problem with children born out of wedlock and then given over to be raised by the mother of the girl who had the child. The origin of the child would become a family secret. Such was Celeste's own case. She had been given to her grandmother to be raised and she was not allowed to know who her father was. This had been true of both her mother and her grandmother.

When we asked the Lord to show us the root cause, He again took us back to life on the plantations of the south during the time of slavery. He showed us a young black girl who had become pregnant by her owner. When the child was born, the family refused to talk to anyone about where the child came from, even though her origin was apparent.

We asked Jesus to come to this young mother and her child, and break the bondage of secrecy in the family. Many children had been born under similar circumstances. Jesus let all of them know that He loved them and that God wanted to be their Father. He then healed the family line of the generational tendency for young women to bear children out of wedlock and to keep the paternity of their children secret.

These are Celeste's own words of another healing episode: "While praying for the generations I became frightened. I felt timid. I wanted to hide. My entire spirit sank. When I asked the Lord why, He took us back to the isle of Barbados. I heard a "roaring" and could not understand why.

The Lord revealed a cave by the ocean. In this cave there was a collection of gentlemen. They turned their backs as Jesus entered the cave. I was appalled that they would turn their backs on the Lord.

It became evident that they were practicing voodoo. I could see the chicken in their hands. I could see them throwing the bones in order to "read" the bones for some form of revelation.

The Lord revealed duplicity. They were professing Christianity and yet they were in darkness, practicing evil. They had been forced into Christianity because they were slaves and they rejected Christ as the white man's God.

They turned their backs, but Christ revealed to them that He knew them and they could not hide from Him. He revealed His love to them. The voodoo priest, who wore an ugly red and black mask, fell at the feet of Christ in tears and adoration. All the gentlemen with him fell at the feet of Christ, praising and worshiping Him in this unusual language.

All through this time there was a pirate watching these gentlemen and Christ. He was entreating these men to continue to practice evil for his own gain. There was no repentance in this man. Christ cut him off from the others and allowed him to go into the darkness.

Praise God for the welcoming of these men into Christ in truth and love. Praise Him for the true revelation of Christ and for the true love that He has for all of mankind, no matter what their racial background!"

Celeste's healing took place over many months. Time after time the feeling would come to me that the problems the Lord showed us were indicative of the problems of most people of color. So at one point I asked her if she would like to have a Eucharist of the generations celebrated for all of the people who had been brought to this country through the slave trade. She agreed and so one Sunday after the regular service we did this.

During the prayers Jesus showed us thousands of people who would be affected by this Eucharist. We felt the terrible pain and burdens of frustration and anger that people of color still experience. This began because of the slave trade which exposed them to captivity and degradation. It continues on today because of the prejudice, poverty, and powerlessness so many experience in our culture.

I felt especially burdened to ask God's forgiveness for the offenses that white people had committed against black people. Then I asked Celeste to forgive me and all of my ancestors for the many ways in which white people had sinned against her ancestors. As she did this we both felt as though strong chains were falling away from our bodies. We saw many, many people kneel down in front of Jesus, white and black alike, and ask forgiveness for the sins they had committed against each other. We have both continued to intercede for the healing that needs to take place among all races of people.

Today Celeste is faced with the challenge of raising her own teenage daughters in the light of the healing and knowledge that the Lord has given her and her family line. As time goes on, she finds herself more and more able to help her own daughters experience the freedom that the Lord has given them to make new choices for living. She is also finding herself free from bondage that was affecting her physical health and her relationships with key men and women in her life.

The Healing of Dale's Family Tree

For a thousand years in your sight are like yesterday when it is past, or like a watch in the night.

Psalm 90:4

This is the story of Dale's healing as told through her own words: "Women in my family drew hurt and weakened men to themselves and then disdained their human weaknesses. My grandfather on mom's side was hurt emotionally in World War I, and my dad experienced the same thing in World War II.

After thoroughly discussing my genogram, we began praying for the Lord Jesus to lead us. My friend and prayer partner, Jean, saw a swinging white door that led to a room with flowery wallpaper.

Pat had me ask Jesus where this was. I waited after asking and received a thought or memory of my grandmother's apartment, which had few windows. I was led to ask Jesus into that apartment. I then walked with Him down the long hall and through rooms where His light shown.

I then remembered my feelings when I was about 7 to 10 years old of not liking to be there. I was led to ask Jesus, 'Why wasn't it a welcoming place?' The response came immediately that my grandparents didn't love each other.

The Lord led through Pat's gentle questions and my verbalizing to Jesus, asking Him into each new 'scene', and then asking Him what to do next. We went back to my grandmother's birth as a result of the question, 'Jesus, why isn't Dale's grandmom loving to her grandfather?' The reply that we heard was, 'Men are weak.' This was from my grandmom's perspective. We asked Jesus where this thought had come from. The questions helped the unfolding of deeper motives and fears in my case and I had a carving out pressure in my chest as I felt my grandmom's shame and guilt. I could actually feel her feelings.

I was asked to identify with my grandmom's actual birth. Her Mom died ten days after her birth. I received a picture of a difficult birth. I verbalized my grandmom's reluctance to be born and cause so much pain to her mom. I could feel her fear in me. This was addressed with words of comfort from Jesus.

Pat suggested I ask Jesus into the bedroom where my grandmom was delivered by her own grandfather (my great-great-grandfather), who was a doctor. The room is very clean. I see Jesus holding my Grandmom as an infant and pray for His love and healing balm upon her. Eventually I see her face relax and she is comforted.

Now I ask Jesus to go to my great-grandmom, who died ten days after her daughter's birth. As Jesus goes to her, my great-grandmom gets up out of the bed and goes off holding Jesus' hand. She looks very peaceful.

Then we see my great-great-grandfather, the doctor, in sorrow with his head down over his daughter's body. We sense that he received ostracism and attacks for somehow bringing about his daughter's death by infection. I'm led to bring Jesus to him for healing and freedom from the heavy guilt he is bearing.

Pat asked if I could see my grandmom as a young girl. I can. I ask Jesus into the scene and as we continue to intercede for her she is able to receive His warmth. I see her smiling and lifting her hands to His light.

We give back to Jesus the judgment, 'Men will fail you.' which I inherited through my mom and my grandmom. We also give to

Him the terrible fear and loneliness and guilt that my grandmom had at bringing pain and death to her mom through her birth. We renounce the lie that was prevalent in my family, that death is icy cold darkness, and receive the truth of death as a transition, taking us to Jesus.

We then went to my father's family line asking for the root cause of the mental illness he suffered from, and of the greed in my aunts and uncles. Piece by piece we saw it. We saw a picture of a dark shadow and asked Jesus to clarify what we were seeing.

I saw faces around a fire and Jean saw a cave and satanic influence. Pat mentioned a tribe coveting what another tribe had and killing for greed. The word 'cannibal' came printed right across my mind's eye. We again asked Jesus to clarify what we were seeing.

We asked Jesus into each of the situations we were seeing to heal them, after He did this Pat was led to do prayer for the removal of the curses of murder, blood guiltiness, satanic involvement, cannibalism, greed, and multiple personality disorders. The sins of those in past generations made it possible for these curses to come into my family line.

Pat celebrated a Eucharistic service to break the hold these sins had on my family line. After that I was led to ask if Jesus would forgive those in past generations for their sinful behavior. As we continued to pray, I saw the white light of Jesus coming against the darkness which resisted Him.

Pat asked me if I could forgive the greed of my aunts and uncles, which stemmed from this root, and I did. Then she prayed healing forgiveness on the entire family line and served notice to Satan that Jesus reigns in them.

Then we saw the Lord move His arm across the scene and all became white. Whatever He chose to do with those ancestors of thousands of years ago, I know that my present family is cleansed and free. Satan no longer has that ground in my family line.

Then I asked Jesus to show me my dad as he is now. His countenance was relaxed and at peace. I asked Jesus to bring me as a little girl into the scene and my dad stretched out his arms to me, and I to him, and we embraced each other."

Joe's Story

> ...for God did not give us a spirit of timidity but a spirit of power and love and self-control.
>
> 2 Timothy 1:7

It was obvious that the man sitting in front of me had a 'spirit of timidity.' He seemed to be a shy, gentle man who was very fearful and ill at ease. His name was Joe. He had been diagnosed as paranoid schizophrenic many years before. He was under a psychiatrist's care, and was taking medication to help with his symptoms. Joe told me that just getting out of bed and going to work each day required courage that he didn't seem to have any more.

His wife said that he had a problem with psychotic thinking, as most schizophrenics do. He was afraid that people were trying to murder him. Joe also had feelings of 'de ja vu'. He was always certain that whatever was happening to him at the present moment had already happened before in exactly the same way.

When he drove to work in the morning, he would be sure that the cars in front of him were exactly the same cars, lined up in the same way, and leaving by the same exit, as the cars that were in front of him yesterday.

Joe was a repairman and when he got to a person's home to do some repair work, he would be sure he had repaired the same item, in the same home, just a short time before. He even had a hard time billing people because he would be sure that it was his work that was defective, until his wife would assure him that he had not done the work before. In the evening, when his children were doing their homework, he would get upset because he would be sure that they had done exactly the same homework the night before and the night before that!

Joe's life was totally disorganized. He was unable to keep records properly and never knew how much people owed him, or whether or not he had enough money to pay his bills. His supplies were also in great disarray and this upset his wife a great deal.

Several people owed Joe large sums of money for work that he had done for them. He would not try to collect this money because of the pervasive fear that colored every moment of his life.

He was in conflict with his sisters and brothers over an inheritance he had received from his parents. He would do nothing to justify his claim because of deep feelings of unworthiness.

As I took Joe's history, I could see that a lot of his problems seemed to be coming from the treatment he received from his family. He had a deep root of bitterness over the way in which they had victimized him. He had been told from the time that he was a small child that he was born to take care of his parents, and they made sure that he fulfilled this role.

He had been abused terribly by his father. He treated Joe as though he was a slave. From the time he was a young boy he had to do all of the work around his home and on rental property they owned, despite the fact that there were six other children in the family. His father abused him further by saying that he would rather have a mentally ill son he could control than a healthy one.

As we made out Joe's genogram we saw additional problems coming down through the generations. There were patterns of alcoholism, incest, adultery, bitterness, and rape coming down through his father's family line. Hoarding of money and goods seemed to be habitual throughout the family line. Along with this there was a general mismanagement of time and money, and a pattern of quarreling over inheritance coming down through his mother's side of the family.

The number of infant deaths was also striking. Within three generations there had been eleven children who were either miscarried or had died during the first year of life. Joe's mother had miscarried a set of twins and allowed the attending doctor to preserve them in formaldehyde in order to use them as scientific specimens.

During our first session of healing of generations prayer we committed all of these lost children into Jesus' arms during the celebration of the Holy Eucharist. As soon as we finished the Eucharist we went into prayer, asking Jesus to heal the sexual problems that seemed to be rampant in Joe's family line.

Jesus took us back many centuries to an old farm where people were engaging in bestiality. When we asked Him what had caused these people to do this, He showed us ancestors who were engaging in satanic worship. Jesus led us to understand that someone in that generation who was actively involved in this satanic worship had invoked a curse of bestiality upon the generations that came after them.

This curse had led members of the family line that gave into it to engage in all kinds of sexual aberrations. The Lord led us to understand that Joe and the other members of his family were in soul-bondage to people in past generations who had practiced bestiality. His brothers had given in to an inner urge to engage in sexual aberrations. From this came the sinful actions of adultery, rape, and incest. Joe had resisted this because of the high moral standards that came from his Christian beliefs, and as a result had a problem with impotency. This problem was gone after our first session.

When we asked Jesus into the terrible scenes we saw, He stopped the people and let us know that he was cutting this sin out of the family line forever. He also led us to understand that there were many curses on Joe's family line because of the sins that his ancestors had engaged in. Some of these curses were the results of their own actions, and some were put upon them by others.

He led us to break curses of blood lust, bestiality, diabolical witchcraft, and death. We felt that these were formal curses that were placed upon the family during the satanic ritual Jesus showed us. So, we broke the curses by declaring them null and void in the name of the Father, Son, and Holy Spirit.

This was repeated three times in this way: "In the Name of the Father, Son, and Holy Spirit, I break the curse of _____ (name the specific curse, such as 'bestiality'). In the Name of the Father, Son, and Holy Spirit, I break the curse of _____. In the Name of the Father, Son, and Holy Spirit, I break the curse of _____, and declare it null and void forever."

I use this formula because very strong curses that come down in a family line, as these had, are very often set in place by being repeated three times in the name of a satanic trinity.

The next time we met, Joe said he felt a lot of relief. However, we knew there were still many problems to tackle. We felt that there were still many curses on this family and so we celebrated the Eucharist a second time in order to break the bondage coming down through the generations.

One of the outstanding problems in his family seemed to stem from their bad financial management and their extremely anxious ways of hoarding. Joe had strong feelings of powerlessness and inadequacy over the handling of his finances. This led him to feel that everything he put his hand to was lost.

As we asked Jesus to show why this was so, we began to see an Irish woman whose family was very hungry. She was hiding food in her apron. Her husband was sitting nearby with his head in his hands, feeling hopeless because he couldn't feed his family. The children were hovering around her, crying for food, but she was afraid to give up what she was hiding.

We began praying for her, but nothing happened until Joe asked Jesus to forgive him for his own habit of hoarding, and for his family's hoarding. Then we saw Jesus come into the picture. After we interceded for this woman for a few minutes, she was able to turn the contents of her apron over to the Lord. There were three pathetic, little, rotten, inedible potatoes that she had been hiding. When she gave to Jesus what little she had, Jesus gave her back an apron full of good food. Then Jesus knelt down next to her and ministered to her. As Joe forgave her on behalf of the generations of his family and asked Jesus to also forgive her, Jesus took her in his arms. He told her how much He loved her. He let her know that He understood her fear.

We then asked Jesus if there was anyone else in the family line who was guilty of hoarding. He showed us a wizened old man who was in a dark little room that was full of coins. The man proceeded to lock the door and began to count his money. He was hoarding these coins because money had become his god. He was a terribly skinny man, almost like a skeleton.

As we interceded for this man, we saw Jesus come into the room with him. The man became blacker. He was furious. There was fire in his eyes. He knew that Jesus was asking him to turn away from the money and accept His love. He had made up his mind that he was not going to part with his money. Jesus began to move closer to him, until He was next to him on the floor. But the man had made a decision that he was not going to surrender to Jesus. The man asked Jesus, "How could You love me?" We felt Jesus was saying, "Because I Am God."

As Joe saw this, he again asked Jesus to forgive him for hoarding his own money, for not giving full tithes to the church, and for not trusting the Lord to provide for the needs of his family. He also asked forgiveness for bad stewardship in not taking care of his money properly, and for letting others bilk him out of his money.

Each time he asked forgiveness of Jesus and sent his forgiveness back to this ancestor we saw the old man healed a little bit, but not totally. Finally, when I commanded the spirit of mammon to leave the family line, the old man threw himself on the floor and began to have a seizure.

At this point I felt that there must be another curse on the family. Jesus led me to believe that the curse was one of financial insecurity. So I again invoked the Trinity and declared the curses of financial insecurity and financial mismanagement broken.

We then had the impression that we were to pray for the tiny hurting child within this man. As we did this we saw Jesus take the child out of the man and hold him and love him. Then Jesus called His mother, Mary. She came into the picture and took this child and began to cuddle him and give him the nurturing love he should have received from his mother.

As Joe sent his forgiveness back to this ancestor and asked Jesus to forgive him, we saw the old man come into the light and give himself to Jesus. Then Jesus again knelt down beside the old man. The man slowly reached up his arm to Jesus and surrendered to Him. Jesus wept tears of love and compassion as the man did this, He washed the man clean with His tears.

Joe and his wife then began to ask Jesus to forgive them for their harsh judgment of his parents because of the way in which they hoarded their money. Then they sent their forgiveness and repentance back to them. We then saw Jesus cut off this curse and its effects on Joe, his wife, his children and all of his siblings.

After this Joe's attitude toward money was much more responsible. He felt more capable of handling his finances wisely. He no longer felt the need to hoard his money, and he was able to begin tithing to his church. Not only did he feel secure about the money he had, but he was now able to collect the money that others owed him.

The next time I prayed for Joe I felt the need to address the soul-bondage he was in. He was in bondage to his mother and father, who were deceased, and to his brothers and sisters, who were still living. We also realized that his wife controlled him greatly. She was quick to accept this and as we prayed she first repented and asked his forgiveness.

We then celebrated the Holy Eucharist for him, asking Jesus to cut off and make null and void any bondage he was in to any person, living or dead, and to strengthen his union with Jesus Christ. After this Joe felt much more freedom from the tension he had always lived with.

The next time that Joe came we again celebrated the Holy Eucharist. This time our prayer was that he would be healed of the disease of schizophrenia. As we prayed for him the Lord took him back to a scene that happened just before he began to have severe emotional problems.

His first episode of schizophrenia came when he had a very high fever during a bout with scarlet fever. During this illness he repeatedly saw a vision of a witch whenever he looked at the light in his bedroom. We asked Jesus to show us what was actually happening. He took us to a scene where a woman dressed in black witches' clothing was standing over a baby and cursing it.

Jesus led us to believe that this woman had caused a curse of mental illness to come upon Joe's family line. There had been someone in each generation with some form of serious mental illness for many generations back. Along with this had come the curse of precognition, or 'de ja vu,' that Joe had problems with for many years.

We declared this curse broken in the name of the Father, Son, and Holy Spirit. We then asked Jesus to come into the scene we were seeing. Jesus confronted the woman with the evil she was doing and she became very contrite and asked His forgiveness. As Joe sent his forgiveness to her and also asked Jesus to forgive her, we saw her clothes turn white. She knelt down in a repentant way and Jesus made a gesture of forgiveness over her head.

We then asked Jesus if this was the only reason for the schizophrenia. He led us to understand that Joe was a very sensitive person who absorbed all of the family's pain and abuse into his inner being. In a sense we felt that Joe was the scapegoat for the other members of his family.

In Old Testament times on the Day of Atonement the priest would symbolically take the sins of the people of Israel and put them onto the back of a goat. This goat would then take away the sins of the people as it was driven out of the camp into the wilderness. This was the 'scapegoat'.

Joe became the scapegoat for all of his family members by taking into himself all of their sin and pain, and paying the price for this through the illness of schizophrenia. He also, unknowingly, took upon himself the curses that had been put upon his family line.

Before we finished with this episode the Lord took us to a memory that had hurt Joe terribly and also contributed greatly to the psychotic thinking that plagued him. He was just a small boy, four or five years old, and he was walking past his parents' bedroom. They had left their door open and Joe, very innocently, looked in. They were having intercourse.

He was transfixed by this strange scene. His father saw him and bellowed at him in rage, making it seem as though Joe were guilty of some terrible indiscretion. He was terror-stricken. He had not meant to do anything wrong and his whole idea of reality was fractured as the father he revered violated his sensitive nature by screaming at him in anger. He never recovered from this incident.

We asked Jesus to come into this scene and heal it. Jesus went to Joe's father and told him that it was wrong for him to treat his son in this way. He told his father to apologize to Joe. He led Joe to understand that what his parents were doing was perfectly normal, but that they were the ones who should have been more discrete. They should have closed their door and secured their privacy.

Jesus then closed the door on Joe's parents and carried him to his own room. There He explained to Joe that his parents had not been able to give him the nurturing he needed because they were both such hurting people. Jesus then asked His parents, Mary and Joseph, to come and spend some time with Joe, giving him the nurturing he should have received from his own parents. We gave Joe a lot of time that day to just enjoy the love and attention of these wonderful parents. When he left, I told him to spend as much time as he could during the next week with Mary and Joseph.

I worked with Joe for one year. During that time I celebrated the Holy Eucharist fourteen times for the healing of his family line. Each time Jesus would show us curses that needed to be broken, and demonic spirits that needed to be cast out of Joe and his family line. We would discern the presence of familiar spirits that corresponded to the curses put on the family line, and to the hurts sustained by people in the past generations. As this happened, I would command these familiar spirits to leave in Jesus' Name and Joe would see Jesus pulling them out of his body. Then we would pray for the places they had been inhabiting to be filled with the Holy Spirit.

Our work did not always center on healing of generations prayer. At times we focused on spiritual direction, helping Joe to learn to get his life in line with Biblical precepts. It was very important to replace the circular thinking that was habitual with him with an understanding of the promises of God, contained in Scripture.

At other times we did some reality counseling. The parenting that Joe had received from his mother and father was so bad that I felt that it was a wonder that Joe even knew how to brush his teeth and blow his nose. The abuse he received from his brothers and sisters made him distrust every decision he made.

Joe made great strides over the year he came to me. He was very anxious to be healed, so he followed my directions well. He went to church regularly and received the Holy Eucharist several times a week. He also received strong support from his wife and friends. These are all necessary conditions for healing a disorder of this magnitude.

A very important ingredient in the healing process is the Body of Christ. People who are in the process of having Jesus heal great hurts need to receive the sacraments regularly. They need the understanding and help of the clergy, and they need the prayerful support of other Christians. Joe had this kind of support and it was an essential part of his healing process.

Finally, we came to the point where Joe felt that he was healed, except for 'a little bit of fear', as he put it. He was also still bothered from time to time by the spirit of precognition. So, with the consent of his psychiatrist, we scheduled a deliverance for the following Saturday. Two tested prayer counselors planned to be on hand to help. We felt that this would be a difficult deliverance because these spirits had been harassing Joe for so long.

We fasted and prayed for Joe ahead of time to receive the strength to do this. On Saturday we first celebrated the Holy Eucharist and then we began the deliverance. It went very well.

Within two hours Jesus had delivered Joe from several spirits, including the major ones of precognition and paranoia, or unreasonable fear. After the deliverance we prayed for Joe to be filled with the Holy Spirit and for all of the portals of his soul and spirit to be sealed, so none of these spirits could come back in again. (See Chapter 9: Deliverance in Generational Healing.)

A few weeks after the deliverance took place Joe called me because the old pattern of fear had returned. As I questioned him about this, it was clear that he was not attempting to keep the spirits out by taking control over them. So I first commanded them to leave, and then I gave him instruction on keeping them out.

Evil spirits always try to harass people for a while after a deliverance. They want to get back into the comfortable home they inhabited for so long. It is necessary for the person delivered to take authority and continue to order them to stop. I told Joe that every time he felt any harassment he should say a prayer of command:

"In the Name of Jesus Christ I command you to get away from me. I belong to Jesus Christ and you can have no place in me."

The next time Joe came to see me he was a changed man. His clothes were neat and his hair was combed. But the smile and the look of peace on his face said the most to me. When I asked how he felt, he was characteristically short. He was "Fine." But his wife added, "He has no more psychotic thinking." I was exuberant!

Can I say that Joe was completely healed of paranoid schizophrenia? No, I can't claim that. I hope that over time his doctor will be able to attest to his complete healing. But I do know that when I last saw him, Joe, like the Gerazene demoniac, was at peace and 'in his right mind.' Praise God!

As I have attempted to indicate, healing of generations prayer alone may not be enough to bring a person with severe problems into healing, no matter how skilled the prayer-counselors. A mixture of prayer, spiritual direction, and counseling is needed.

Sometimes these different approaches can be utilized by one prayer-team, at other times it is better to refer the people to others for continuing therapy. Sometimes the people who come to us are simply not ready for a ministry of this type.

They may need the help of a psychiatrist or a psychotherapist. They may need a self-help program, such as Alcoholics Anonymous, Alanon, or Incest Survivors Anonymous. They may need to work with these people for a few months or a few years before they are ready for healing of generations.

However, I truly believe that the time will come when they can benefit greatly from this ministry. We need to have the patience and the wisdom to allow this to happen at the right time. Healing is a process. It begins when people desire healing so much that they are willing to go back into the great pain that is coming down through their family line in order to receive it. It continues to take effect as they work to let go of any anger and bitterness they may have, and as they become ready to forgive those who hurt them and the members of their families. As they make a decision to give up self-pity and take charge of their own lives, they begin to put aside bad habits and thought patterns and replace them with Christian ways of thinking and living. The process is completed as they become willing to stand up and take charge of their own lives, always leaning on the love of Christ and the power of the Holy Spirit to enable them in their journey toward wholeness.

There are many more case histories that I could recount here, but I chose these three because they were each unique. Each showed strongly the desire of our Lord to heal and set His people free from the bondage coming down through the generations.

They show the love of a Savior bent on freeing His people from generations of pain and sin. They emphasize how important it is for us to remember and have faith in these two things: Jesus has both the *desire* and the *power* to bring His people into total and complete healing of mind, body, and spirit. Praise God for His wondrous love!

Part 3

Power

to

Heal

Chapter Eight

The Healing Power of the Holy Eucharist

> For I received from the Lord what I also handed onto you, that the Lord Jesus on the night when He was betrayed took bread, and when He had given thanks, He broke it and said, "This is my body which is for you. Do this in remembrance of me." In the same way also the cup, after supper, saying, "This cup is the new covenant in my blood. Do this, as often as you drink it, in remembrance of me."
>
> 1 Corinthians 11:26

As I stated in Chapter 6, the more experience we have in praying with people for generational healing, the more we find that some things in the family line simply will not be solved by intercessory prayer alone. These are actions so sinful, hurts so deep that only the greatest power available to the Christian will heal them. This is the power that is present to us in the celebration of the Holy Eucharist.

Those who are deeply involved in praying for others for healing of generations have learned that the Sacrament of the Holy Eucharist (also known as the Lord's Supper, the Liturgy of the Mass, or Holy Communion) holds the central place in this ministry. God has shown us that through the redemptive power present in the Holy Eucharist, and through the strong intercessory prayer of deeply committed Christians, we may appropriate all of the benefits of Christ's passion, death, and resurrection to heal ancestral wounds.

As an Episcopal priest, I have found that the most important thing I can do for those who come to me for the healing of generations is to offer this sacramental way of healing to them. I see the Eucharist as the dynamite that breaks up what appears to be an immovable rock of hurt and sin that is blocking the healing of the family line. As the Eucharist is celebrated, this rock is broken apart and the problems that caused it become accessible to our prayers. We then receive discernment about where to direct our petitions.

I celebrate the Holy Eucharist for the healing of the family lines of each person who comes to me. I do this after the initial interview with the supplicant and before beginning intercessory prayer for those in the family lines. In this way, I feel the healing power of the Holy Eucharist is used to best advantage, as it breaks the bondage that the pain and sin of past generations has put upon the family lines.

The Power of Jesus' Sacrifice

The concept of the transformation of time (Chapter 5) is a key to understanding the action of God during the healing of the generations. It is also central to understanding what is happening during the celebration of the Holy Eucharist. As the Eucharist is celebrated on behalf of the past generations of the supplicant's family lines, all of the power of God that was used in the creation of the world and in the raising of Jesus from the grave is poured into all of the hurting places in the ancestral line.

Through the atoning power of Jesus' sacrificial death, made present through the Eucharist, bondage is broken that may have been in the family lines for centuries. Sins are forgiven and people are set free from their hurts. We have seen whole families changed when this has occurred.

When Jesus died, His shed blood paid the price for our sins. That was the most powerful moment in the history of the world. In that moment, Satan, the vicious enemy of all humankind, was completely and irrevocably defeated. Satan went down to defeat as Jesus uttered His last cry upon the cross, "It is finished." Three days later, Jesus rose from the dead in God's triumph over death. He opened the gates of eternal life to all who would believe in Him. Thus He became the living bridge for forgiveness of sins between God, who is ultimate good, and all of humankind, who had been lost to Him through sin and death.

As St. Paul wrote:

> Death is swallowed up in victory.
> O death, where is thy victory?
> O death, where is thy sting?'
> The sting of death is sin, and the power of sin is the law. But thanks be to God, who gives us the victory through our Lord Jesus Christ.

> 1 Corinthians 15:53b-54

When we celebrate the Holy Eucharist on behalf of those who sinned in past generations, we appropriate the awesome power of God that triumphed over sin and death for ourselves and our forebears. In the Eucharist, time is transformed and all of sacred history becomes one with and in the present moment.

We are with God at the moment of creation. We are with Abraham as he takes Isaac up the holy mountain in obedience to God's command. We are with Moses as he leads the Israelite people out of Egypt and through the waters of hope.

We are with Mary as she yields her entire being to God, so that His Spirit may plant the seed of the Holy Child within her. We walk the dusty roads of Palestine with a ragtag band of men who feel that they have found the long-awaited Messiah.

We are with Jesus as He teaches and heals, as He is betrayed by Judas, and as He hangs in agony upon the cross. We are there when His lifeless body is laid to rest, and we feel the power of new life as He bursts from the tomb on that first Easter morning. The future also becomes one with this moment as the final judgement becomes present to us.

> In the act of worship, we come into the presence of God. In the ecstasy of prayer, our spirits are caught up in God's spirit. Since God is equally present at all times and in all places in the spirit, our time in particular is contemporary with that time in which the decisive revelation of God appeared.

> 'Were you there when they crucified my Lord?
> Were you there when they nailed him to the tree?
> Were you there when they laid him in the tomb?'

> The answer implied is Yes! And we were there also when God raised him from the dead, and when he sat at God's right hand.[1]

As we stand in God's presence during a Eucharistic celebration for the healing of the generational sins and hurts in our family line, all of the healing power of those most precious deeds are ours anew. In the timelessness of God, every event that has ever taken place in our family history is present, and He can bring to our minds any one of those events that needs His healing touch.

Anamnesis

A greater perception of what is actually happening during a celebration of the Holy Eucharist comes through understanding the full meaning of the word, *remembrance*, as it was used by Jesus during the Last Supper and is used today during the Eucharistic prayer of consecration, "Do this in remembrance of me."

Jesus during the Last Supper and is used today during the Eucharistic prayer of consecration, "Do this in remembrance of me."

The word *remembrance* is a translation of the Greek word, *anamnesis. Anamnesis* means to remember something that happened in the past in such a way that it actually becomes present to us today with the same living force that it had when it first occurred.

Every Eucharist is an anamnesis, a re-presentation of the passion, death, and resurrection of our Lord Jesus Christ. Therefore each Eucharist that is celebrated has within it each and every benefit of those mighty acts of God by which He set us free from our sins and offered us eternal life in His kingdom.

Thus, the words, "Do this in remembrance of me," are not just a reminder of an action done thousands of years ago, when Jesus presided over a meal with His followers and told them of His approaching death. As we say these words, we are recalling again the passion, death, and resurrection of Jesus Christ in such a way that these events are actually with us once again. They become present to us each time we take part in a Eucharistic celebration and each time they have all of the reality and living power that they had in Jerusalem two thousand years ago.

The Theological Word Book of the Bible offers this explanation:

When therefore Jesus said, "Do this in remembrance of me" (1 Cor. 11.24), he was assuredly not planning merely to keep before his disciples' minds that which they could anyhow never forget; it was to be a 'concrete remembering', a bringing back out of the past into the present - of what? Not of sins, for by his sacrifice they are taken away. But of the sacrifice itself, or rather of *him*, crucified, risen from the dead, victorious through death. As he at the Last Supper, taking his bread and wine, identified them with his body and blood, as the liturgical emblems of his sacrifice; so they, afterward, taking their bread and wine, would do with them what he had done 'in objective-remembrance of him.'. Then he, in the power of

Healing of generations has all of the elements of this type of remembering in it. Each time we engage in prayer for our family line is a time of anamnesis. As we pray for the healing of ancestral bondage, Jesus brings into the present moment all of the hurting and sin-filled moments of our family history. As He does this, He releases into those wounds the healing power of His presence, just as He does during the Eucharist.

This is true whenever we go into prayer. Every time we go to Jesus in prayer and ask for His healing touch on a person or situation, He meets us, and at that moment He is as present with us as He was with His disciples when He talked with them on the mountain, or walked with them on the shores of the Sea of Galilee. And whenever we meet together with Christ Jesus all of the power that was His to heal the sick or to calm the stormy sea is present to us in all of its fullness.

This is especially so during the Holy Eucharist, because during the Eucharist we celebrate the passion, death, and resurrection of our Lord Jesus Christ. By His death, Jesus broke the power that sin and death had over us. He delivered us from the domain of Satan and brought us into oneness with God,

> "...for he is the true Paschal Lamb, who was sacrificed for us, and has taken away the sin of the world. By his death he has destroyed death, and by his rising to life again he has won for us everlasting life."[3]

Not only is Christ present each time we partake of the Holy Eucharist, "in the power of His accepted sacrifice," but all of the benefits accrued to us by those redemptive acts become ours as well. Christ's death paid the full price for our sins, breaking the hold that Satan had on all of humankind. Now, those who accept Jesus as Savior and Lord are freed forever from the tyranny of sin.

His resurrection opened to us the gates of heaven and put eternity within our grasp. Thus the gift of eternal life is offered to all who would follow Him.

The power of this sacrifice is not lost on our adversary; who holds those who have sinned greatly in our ancestral line in his grip. So one of the reasons we celebrate the Holy Eucharist for the generations of a family is to serve notice that he no longer has power over them. Their bondage is broken and they are transferred from the enemy's domain into the hands of God through the completed sacrifice of Jesus Christ, and through the sacrificial prayers of the members of the present generation.

During a Holy Eucharist celebrated for the healing of a person's family lines that same power that tore the sins of human beings off of their backs now breaks the bonds of death and sin that have been holding our ancestors and our present-day families captive. That power enlivens and strengthens His people, enabling them to follow in His footsteps of sacrificial love.

It strengthens, heals, and makes new all who would do the hard work of bringing the generations of their families into healing through the cross of Jesus Christ. There is more of God's power and love available in and to His people during the celebration of the Holy Eucharist than we can ever comprehend, or that is ever available to us at any other time or in any other way.

This is so because when we celebrate the Holy Eucharist with the intention of breaking the hold that sin has upon our forebears, whether they lived before the time of Christ or after His coming, we put up against the evil that they have done that wonderful and awesome 'good' of God that through His Son, Jesus Christ, triumphed over sin and death.

As the Eucharist is celebrated to break the hold that sin has on our ancestral lines, God releases His love and forgiveness into each and every hurting place. All of sacred history becomes one with and in the present moment as we actively participate in a moment of remembrance that has the potential to heal, strengthen, and make new all who participate in it *and* all of the wounded places in the family lines that we bring to it. This concept stands as the most important part of our understanding about the transformation of time during prayers for the healing of generations.

A Ministry for All Members of the Church Lay and Ordained

In putting such a strong emphasis on the celebration of the Holy Eucharist, I do not mean to imply that those who minister healing of generations must be ordained clergy. This is definitely a ministry that lay people and clergy should be carrying on together.

If you are a lay person, ask your pastor if he or she is willing to celebrate a Eucharist regularly at a prearranged time for all of those coming to you for the healing of generations. This could be a regularly scheduled midweek service or a service held specifically for healing of generations. It could be public or private. It could be held once a week or once a month. The important thing is that the Eucharist is held with the intention of breaking the bondage coming down from past generations of a family line.

If you cannot find a clergy person who is willing to celebrate the Eucharist for you, receive as much healing prayer as you can with a prayer counselor, then take your family chart to a regularly scheduled celebration of the Eucharist and ask the Lord to apply the benefits of that Eucharist for the healing of any person or problem in your family line. God will never leave us without the healing we need because of a lack that we are not able to fulfill, but will always work His healing power within the circumstances of our lives!

Preparing to Celebrate the Holy Eucharist

As we prepare to celebrate the Holy Eucharist for the healing of generations, we make out our generational charts, or genograms. We look at them prayerfully and candidly, asking the Holy Spirit to make clear to us what problem, person, or particular group of people, need our prayers the most at this time. Follow the discernment the Lord gives to you. There may be a problem that is uppermost in your mind, or there may be something hidden in the generations that you know nothing about. The good news is that God knows! As we go to Him in prayer for the needs of our family lines He will show us where to begin, if we allow Him to.

The following account is an example of the things that are unknown until we ask the Holy Spirit to shine His light into our family's past. As you can imagine, I have already had much healing prayer for my family lines. However, I recently took part in a conference that Dr. Kenneth McAll gave and received much more healing. At the closing Eucharist, Dr. McAll instructed us to make out our family tree and pray over it to see what Jesus wanted to heal, before placing it on the altar for prayer.

As I did this, I realized that I had never really prayed for the different national groups that my ancestors represented. I wrote down their names and how I felt they had impacted others. Then I asked Jesus to forgive them for any hurt they had caused.

I began to concentrate on my mother's family line. As I did this, I was aware of the figure of my grandmother, standing off to one side, almost covered in dark shades of brown. The fact that my grandmother's ancestors were Scotch-Irish came into my mind.They came from warlike clans, always doing battle with one another. At one point in time they emigrated to Northern Ireland.

At this point, the Lord brought another part of my grandmother's ancestry into my mind. She was very proud that she was a descendant of those who were responsible for Ireland coming under British rule. As I prayed about this I could still see my grandmother's figure in darkness in the foreground, but behind her I could see the Irish people fighting my ancestors who had settled on their lands so many years before and been responsible for so much of their past and present pain.

I began to ask Jesus to forgive all of these ancestors for so selfishly and thoughtlessly taking authority over the lands and fortunes of the Irish people. As I did this I first saw them fighting together over the land. Then as I continued to ask forgiveness for the deeds of my ancestors, I began to see Jesus among them, bringing them together in understanding and forgiveness. He then held His hand up in the air. As He did this, I saw living waters stream from His hand down through all of Ireland, bathing all of these people in His love. They stopped their fighting, and were washed in these heavenly waters. As this happened they began to playfully throw water on one another, and were soon frolicking together in the water, having a great time, laughing and crying all at the same time.

Then I saw my grandfather join my grandmother. Their figures became white as they turned to Jesus and went off with Him, hand in hand. I had the feeling that my grandmother and my grandfather had been praying for this to happen for a long time. I felt a great sense of release, of something finally falling into place in my spirit, as this happened. Since that time I have felt much more at peace with myself and my lineage. I write this account so that others will understand how important it is to take the time before the Eucharist to pray for more enlightenment into the problems coming down through the generational lines, even when at first glance there doesn't seem to be anything outstanding.

Here are some suggestions given to me by the Rev. Frank Santilli, a Roman Catholic Priest from Pawtucket, R.I. I hope they will help as you make out your genogram:

1. Identify, by name, the people in your family who . . .

- Were very superstitious, involved in pagan worship, cults, or the occult.
- Died in tragic ways (e.g., suicide, accident, murder, etc.).
- Had miscarriages, abortions, or stillborn babies.
- Died without being committed to God, or feeling unloved or abandoned (e.g., in a mental institution, nursing home, prison, etc.).
- Were considered outcasts, rejects, or black sheep.
- Had a problem with addictions (e.g., food, alcohol, drugs, work, etc.).
- Were depressed, angry, bitter, unforgiving, vengeful.
- Were involved in sexual perversions (e.g., adultery, pornography, prostitution, incest, etc.).

2. Identify what you would consider to be "patterns" of sin in your family tree, for instance:

- anger   temper   physical abuse   sexual abuse   promiscuity
- holding grudges   racial prejudices   unforgiveness   revenge murder   arrogance   jealousy   materialism   greed   lust

3. What health problems seem to be prominent in your family, for instance:

- cancer   heart trouble   high blood pressure   diabetes
- arthritis   skin problems   respiratory trouble   headaches
- mental retardation   mental disturbances   ulcers
- psychological problems   nervous breakdowns   forgetfulness

As you meditate on these questions, ask the Lord where the problems that surface had their beginning in your family lines. As you prepare to take part in the generational liturgy offer them to God for healing.

As we continue our preparations for the Eucharist of the Generations, this becomes a time of strong intercession for those in past generations, as we ask our Lord to gather them together where they can see Him as Savior and Redeemer. During this time, we purposefully ask God to use us as conduits of His love and power in order that all of those in our family lines may be freed from any kind of bondage to pain or sin. We ask Him to reveal and break any curses that might hold our present generation in bondage.

As I emphasized earlier, we also ask Him to forgive the people in each generation who have sinned greatly, giving the names when known. Then we send our forgiveness back to those in past generations on behalf of all of our family members, living and dead. At this point we also need to ask Jesus' forgiveness for any way in which we may have given in to the temptation to sin in the same way as past generations have. At the offertory, the generational chart can be put on the altar and all of the family lines, past, present and future, can be lifted up to Jesus for healing and wholeness.

Here are some further suggestions for your use as you participate in the celebration of the Holy Eucharist for the healing of your family line. These were given to me by the Rev. Robert Kerner, an Episcopal priest from Georgia:

As you enter into the celebration of the Eucharist, take the person(s) with you into prayer. At the various parts of the Mass, offer specific prayers for them; for example:

1.   At the Penitential Rite . . . stand in for them and for your whole family, asking the Lord's mercy and forgiveness.

2.   During the Liturgy of the Word, ask that the power of the Word of God may be directed to the deceased and to the living for whom you are praying.

3.   At the Presentation and Offering of the gifts of bread and wine, offer up to the Lord the lives of those for whom you are praying; see them being raised up to the Father with the offerings of bread and wine.

4.   During the Eucharistic Prayer, pray that the deceased are transformed as the gifts of bread and wine are transformed into the Body and Blood of Jesus.

5.   In the power of the Spirit, pray the words of the Lord's Prayer for them.

6.   As you process up to the Altar to receive Holy Communion, take the deceased with you in your heart and receive for yourself and for them in a holy communion.

7.   After Communion, give thanks for the gifts of your departed and for the life of Christ that is flowing through you and them.

8.   At the end of the service, break ties with them and release them into Jesus' hands. Give thanks to Him for all He has done.

Sometimes the Eucharist for the healing of generations needs to be repeated several times for one family line. This may be true when people have difficult problems, such as incest or schizophrenia. The root causes of these illnesses may be curses or pacts that were placed upon the family by those in past generations who were engaging in extremely evil practices, such as pagan or satanic worship.

A Time of Worship, Adoration, and Great Healing

The principle of any liturgy is to worship, adore, and proclaim the glory of the Lord God Almighty and His Son Jesus Christ through the power of the Holy Spirit. When celebrating a Eucharist for the healing of generations I always keep this in mind, along with the knowledge that we are also serving notice to the adversary that Jesus Christ has already won the battle against "Satan and all the spiritual forces of wickedness that rebel against God".[4] Thus, during this service we use canticles, psalms, lessons, and prayers that remind us of the truth that Jesus Christ is Lord of lords, and King of kings. He is the King Who reigns!

I like to begin this service with a canticle or sacred song in which we lift up our praises and proclaim the glory of the Holy Trinity, such as the Gloria in Excelsis, or the Te Deum laudamus.[4] Then I lead the congregation in a short prayer that does three things; it expresses our belief in God's will to restore all creation to wholeness in Christ, it proclaims the Lordship of Jesus Christ over all things in heaven and on earth, and it states the reason for our actions, which is to free the past and present generations of our families from their bondage to evil and sin. This is well stated in the Collect of the Reign of Christ.[5] As you will see in the service outline, I have added to its content in order to bring in the needs of the family lines we are praying for.

For the same reasons we most often use the lessons that have been appointed to celebrate the reign of Christ. These lessons are Daniel 7:9-14, Revelation 19:11-16, and John 18:33-37.

If there were many people in the family who died without being committed to the Lord (as might be true of miscarriages, abortions, suicides, violent deaths, or with great sinners of past generations) we might begin the service with the Burial Office (BCP, 491) and use the following lessons: Ezekiel 34:11-17 or Isaiah 25:6-9 for the Old Testament reading; Revelations 21:2-7 or Colossians 1:11-20 for the Epistle; John 6:37-40 or 14:1-6 for the Gospel.

Following the lessons we say the Renunciation of Occult involvement and Reaffirmation of Baptismal Promises together. Then we offer a litany for the healing of the generations. It should be said slowly and thoughtfully, giving time for people to add their personal prayers and for the Holy Spirit to bring specific problems to mind that can then be added to the litany.

A "gathering prayer" from Dr. McAll's book, *Healing the Family Tree,* may be used at the beginning of the service, or at the Offertory:

God our Father in Heaven, we bow in your Presence and thank you for sparing Your only Son.
We know that You, our Lord Jesus Christ, are risen from the dead. You are alive and here with us. Please do You now direct Your angels to gather all our deceased that seem to be lost, especially _____ and many others whom You know but whom we have omitted. Bring them where You wish that they may see Your broken body, healed and risen so that in their brokenness they too might rise. Let them receive Your Blood poured out, a completed act for the forgiveness of their sins.
Bind and banish Satan and his minions to their appropriate place. Let the Body and Blood of our Lord heal all the wounds and torments inflicted by Satan and his minions on the living and the dead.
Father, we come as stumbling children who neither understand nor know how to pray. Send Your Holy Spirit to intercede for us.
We ask this in the Name of our Lord Jesus Christ-Amen.[6]

Another prayer that might be used at the Offertory is the following:

"This Eucharist is offered to the glory of God, with prayers that all of the members of the family lines represented here, living and deceased, may come to know and accept the healing and wholeness offered through Jesus Christ our Lord. Amen."

On the following pages are the service outline and litany that I use for a celebration of the Holy Eucharist for the healing of generations. I hope they will be of benefit to others who lead or participate in this type of healing prayer.

A Celebration of the Holy Eucharist for the Healing of Generations

Celebrant: Blessed be God, Father, Son, and Holy Spirit.
Response: And blessed be His Kingdom, now and forever. Amen.

The Collect for Purity

Gloria in excelsis   (or Kyrie eleison)

Collect: (together) Almighty and everlasting God, whose will it is to restore all things in your well-beloved Son, the King of kings and Lord of lords: mercifully grant that the generations of the families we bring before you now, who have been divided and enslaved by sin and hurt, may be freed and brought together under His most gracious rule; who lives and reigns with you and the Holy Spirit, one God, now and forever.
Amen.

Old Testament lesson:	Daniel 7:9-14
Epistle:	Revelation 19:11-16
The Gospel:	John 18:33-37

Renunciation of Occult Involvement and Reaffirmation of Baptismal Promises   (Appendix B)

The Healing of Generations Litany   (Page 148,149,150)

The Peace.

The Offertory: (Genograms may now be placed on the altar.)

The Great Thanksgiving, Eucharistic Prayer D   (BCP, p. 372)

Post-communion prayer: (together) Almighty God, we thank you for feeding us with the spiritual food of the most precious Body and Blood of our Savior Jesus Christ. May it strengthen and uplift us in our search for wholeness, that we may be able to love you and serve you as living members of the Body of your Son, Jesus Christ, and heirs of your eternal kingdom. To Father, Son, and Holy Spirit be all glory, honor and praise, now and forever. Amen.

The Litany

Almighty and everlasting God, please gather together all of the generations of our family lines, past, present, and future, that they may be healed of all hurts and freed from all bondage.

>Lord, in your mercy, hear our prayer.

We thank you for all of those in our family lines who passed down to us peace, love, and an ability to know you and your Son, Jesus Christ.

>Lord, in your mercy, hear our prayer.

Please send the light of your son, Jesus Christ, into all of the sinful and hurting places in the past generations of our family lines, that people in the past and present generations may know the harm that they have done and come before you with repentant hearts.

>Lord, in your mercy, hear our prayer.

Those in past generations may have suffered pain and grief at the hands of others. Please send the blood of Jesus, shed for the forgiveness of sins, back into all pain-filled and grieving places, that both perpetrators and victims may be forgiven, healed, and freed in Jesus' Holy Name.

>Lord, in your mercy, hear our prayer.

Those in past generations may have sinned against you and hurt others by engaging in occult practices, pagan and satanic worship, and all of the abominations associated with these practices. Please forgive them and break the hold these sinful practices have on our family lines.

>Lord, in your mercy, hear our prayer.

Those in past generations may have sinned against you and hurt others through physical, sexual, or emotional abuse. Please forgive them and break the hold these sins have on our family lines.

>Lord, in your mercy, hear our prayer.

Those in past generations may have sinned against you and hurt others by holding onto anger, unforgiveness and unrepentant bitterness. Please forgive them and break the hold these sins have on our family lines.

Lord, in your mercy, hear our prayer.

Those in past generations may have sinned against you and hurt others by committing suicide, murder, or abortion. Please forgive them and break the hold these sins have on our family lines.

Lord, in your mercy, hear our prayer.

We commend into your hands those in our family lines who committed suicide, were stillborn, aborted, or died untimely deaths, especially__ __(names)___. Receive them into the arms of your mercy, into the blessed rest of everlasting peace, and into the glorious company of the saints in light.

Lord, in your mercy, hear our prayer.

We send our love and forgiveness back to those who hurt members of our family lines. We also send our love and forgiveness back to those members of our family lines who hurt others. We ask you to forgive them and bring them into wholeness and newness of life with you.

Lord, in your mercy, hear our prayer.

We ask you to forgive those of us in this present generation and our progeny for any way in which we may have given in to the tendency to sin in the same way as our forebears did. Forgive us and restore us to life and health.

Lord, in your mercy, hear our prayer.

We offer prayers for those past and present family members who are in special need of your healing touch: _____ (names)_____ .

Lord, in your mercy, hear our prayer.

All: In the Name of Jesus Christ and by the power of His cross and blood, we now break and make null and void any curses, contracts, covenants, hexes, spells, or pacts made against our family lines, or by any member of our family lines against another person. We break and make null and void any inner vows and any bitter root judgements or expectations made against our family lines, or by any member of our family lines against another person. We place the cross and blood of Jesus, the symbols of His power and authority, between the past generations of our families and the present generation, thereby cutting off any evil that could in any way harm them in Jesus' Name. Amen.

Celebrant: Almighty Father, we ask that you reveal to us any places in our family lines that need further prayers. Break the bondage of sin and ignorance. Look upon all of the people in our generational lines with compassion. Free them all, living and dead, that they might come before you in a sure knowledge of your love and forgiveness. Send into every dark and hurting place the love of your Son Jesus Christ, that those in the past, present, and future generations may learn to live in wholeness of mind, body, and spirit, to the eternal glory of your Holy Name, in and through your Son, our Lord Jesus Christ. Amen.

Chapter Nine

Deliverance During Healing of Generations

He has delivered us from the dominion of darkness and transferred us into the kingdom of His beloved Son, in whom we have redemption, the forgiveness of sins.

Colossians 1:13,14

There is sometimes a need for deliverance when doing prayers for the healing of generations. Usually celebrating the Eucharist for the family lines and healing the root cause is enough to make the harassing spirits leave. At other times they have gained a stronger foothold because of subsequent hurts in the family line and the hurting memories of the supplicant. These have to be healed before the spirits will leave. Often you will see Jesus remove them as soon as the hurt that allowed them in is healed.

At times what seems like a strong reaction to an inner hurt, or even a predisposition to sin in a certain way, is in reality harassment or temptation that is coming from an evil spirit. This in no way excuses us when we give in to the temptation. We still have free will and are each responsible for our own actions, no matter how much we are hurt or tempted. However, demonic harassment does make it harder for us to resist the temptations that come our way.

The first sign that a person needs deliverance may come during a prayer session when every attempt to bring healing to the situation seems to be blocked, no matter what methods are used.

The supplicant may not be able to see anything. If the supplicant is able to see a hurting situation, he cannot sense any healing coming to it. His perception of Jesus may be warped. That is, he may see Jesus doing something that is totally out of character, such as standing by while someone is being hurt and not stopping the perpetrators. This is a signal to me that the supplicant has picked up a false view of Jesus somewhere, possibly from a harassing spirit. Another sign of harassment might come when a person is unwilling or unable to forgive those who hurt him, or those who had hurt people in the past generations of his family.

Familiar Spirits

The Son of God was revealed for this purpose, to destroy the works of the devil.

1 John 3:8

The same root causes that I outlined in Chapter 4 as the sources of the problems coming down through the generations are almost always the sources of the demonic activity in family lines. These evil spirits came in when ancestors turned away from God, whether that was through fear, grief, anger or because of a deep inner wound coming from another person's violent action against them. They came in great numbers, and with a deadly grip, if ancestors began to worship other gods and take part in occult, pagan, or satanic activity. The spirits that entered the family line because of these aberrations are the most difficult to expel because they have come from the very place of evil, and have probably had their hooks into the family line for a very long time.

But, as soon as the supplicant renounces the activity of the ancestors whose involvement allowed them in, and takes the advice in the Epistle of James, "But ask in faith, never doubting . . . " (James 1:6), the spirits are on their way out.

Many times harassing spirits pass down through a family line from one generation to another, until someone turns to God for help. I call the spirits that come down through the family line "familiar" spirits. Most of them have been in the family line for a long, long time. Some of these familiar spirits can cause problems such as alcoholism, repeated cases of adultery or incest, rage, or unforgiveness. Some of these spirits have come into the family line through curses that have been placed on a family member, and some come from sins that family members have been habitually engaged in.

A Familiar Spirit of Adultery

Discipline yourselves, keep alert. Like a roaring lion your adversary the devil prowls around, looking for someone to devour. Resist him, steadfast in your faith . . .

1 Peter 5:8,9

An example of this was a woman who came to me with a spirit of adultery. As we prayed for Jesus to show us where this spirit had come into the family line, He took us back through the generations to a scene where one of her ancestors became involved with a married woman. He justified this relationship by saying that his wife was not responsive to his emotional needs. He continued to engage in this sinful behavior, no matter how much this hurt his wife and children. He thus made an opening in himself where the spirit of adultery could come in and take possession. This spirit of adultery continued to pass down through the generational lines vertically, from one generation to the next, such as from father to child. It also passed through the generations horizontally, as from sister to brother, or from cousin to cousin. It had become very *familiar* with this particular family.

The woman who came for healing of generations had inherited the spirit of adultery from her father. A divisive spirit had come in along with it. When she was ten years old, she was already adept at getting in between people and breaking up their relationships. By the time she was eighteen she had begun having affairs with married men. I remember her stating when she first came to see me that she had come to the realization that her "sexual preference" was adultery.

She had just given her life to Jesus and she did not want to do anything that would come between the relationship she was now developing with Him. She made a full confession of her transgressions and then came to me for healing prayer.

The confession was very important because many times evil spirits come into a family line, or an individual, and stay because of a certain inherited pattern of sinfulness. These spirits are very difficult to expel, unless the person goes to Jesus asking for reconciliation. When this happens the evil spirits have lost their hold and must leave.

When we asked Jesus to heal the problem in this woman's life, He first took us back into the generations and healed the root cause. Then He took us to incidents in her father's life that allowed the spirits to enter his generation, and brought them into healing. After that, He brought His forgiveness and healing love to bear on her own life and thus broke the pattern of adultery on the whole family line. When this was accomplished, she was easily delivered of the spirits of divisiveness and adultery.

Turn to Jesus

Submit yourselves therefore to God. Resist the devil and he will flee from you.

James 4:7

As you can see, evil spirits may begin to harass people when they have been deeply hurt themselves, or when they have lived in a family system that was greatly laden with deep hurts and sinful life-patterns coming down from past generations. It is almost as though these problems make a break in our spiritual protection and evil spirits come in to piggyback on the hurts coming from them.

When the person affected turns to Jesus for help and begins to receive enough healing to have faith in His love, the evil spirit is really on its way out. It cannot live for long in someone who has faith in Jesus Christ and submits to the authority that Jesus has as the incarnate Son of God.

In fact, some of the presenting problems that bring people to seek the healing of generations are really just the death throes of familiar spirits who know that their time is up. A person who has his eyes set on Jesus and his heart set on doing His will, will not give familiar spirits room in his life for long.

This explains what is happening to most of the people who come to see me. They may not become aware of the spiritual problems of their ancestors until they become committed Christians. As they begin to live more Christ-centered lives and desire to serve Jesus wholeheartedly, they also become more aware of the enemy's work in their own lives and in the members of their families.

The familiar spirits cannot stand to see Christians become strong. As Christians continue to seek the healing and wholeness that Jesus offers, the enemy's forces will begin to bother them more. But this harassment will be quickly ended once the root cause of the hurt or sin that allowed them entrance into the family line is healed and deliverance prayer is administered.

Back to Root Causes!

..for the weapons of our warfare are not merely human, but they have divine power to destroy strongholds.

2 Corinthians 10:4

When I feel a person is under oppression from evil spirits, the first thing I do is celebrate the Holy Eucharist for the past and present generations of that person's family lines. This sacrament effectively loosens the grip that the enemy has on the family line and on the supplicant. Sometimes this has such a powerful effect that the person experiences a spontaneous deliverance during the celebration.

As I have stated before, I never work alone. This is especially important when doing deliverance, because during deliverance prayer we need more spiritual power and discernment. After celebrating the Eucharist, we go into prayer, looking for the root cause of the problem. As we ask, Jesus will show us what the deep hurt or sin was that allowed this spirit to gain entry into the afflicted one's family line. When we come to an understanding of what the hurt was, we then ask Jesus to come into the situation that caused it and bring it into healing, just as we do in any other episode of generational healing.

Most harassing spirits will leave spontaneously as soon as Jesus brings healing into the situation through which they gained entrance. We will know this has happened because the person will react in some way, either by coughing, or belching, or by exhaling deeply. If we feel the supplicant will be frightened if we mention deliverance prayer, we bind the spirits in Jesus' name and cast them out under our breath. We will know this has been effective because of the change we will see in the supplicant.

If the supplicant was having trouble visualizing a hurting situation, the scene Jesus is showing us will become clearer. If he or she was not able to understand why the hurt occurred, this will now be understood. If the supplicant was not able to forgive, he or she will now be able to at least attempt to forgive the ones who caused the pain. This will tell us that our deliverance prayer was successful, even though the supplicant was not aware that we were praying.

There are other times when either the ancestors of the supplicant engaged in extremely sinful behavior, or a person in the present generation was extremely hurt. These problems allowed evil spirits to gain a strong foothold. Because of them, we have to do the more direct form of deliverance described below.

As Jesus brings the root cause into healing, He also gives us discernment as to the spirits that came into the family line because of it. As in the rest of this ministry, the important thing in deliverance is to always watch Jesus and listen closely to what He is telling you. As you listen to Him, He will give you an inner knowledge of the nature of the spirits that are plaguing the person you are praying for, so that you will know their names. It is important to call them by name as you order them to leave the supplicant.

Their names usually describe their activity. So if the family was indulging in occult practices, then an occult spirit may have come down through the generations. If they have always felt fearful or inadequate, then spirits of fear and inadequacy may be bothering them. If a person has extremely low self-esteem, it may be that a spirit of low self-esteem, or a spirit of lies, is behind this. Mockery often piggybacks on lies, so, many times both of them are together and both will have to be cast out before the supplicant can be free of either one of them.

Some spirits have proper names. These are generally controlling spirits that come from a curse that was put on the family line in the past, sometimes many generations ago.

The Prayer of Command

I will do whatever you ask in My Name, so that the Father may be glorified in the Son.

John 14:12

Once we know the name of the spirit, we must bind it in the Name of Jesus, and command it to leave the person we are praying for and all of the generations of that person's family line. Do not be afraid to take the spiritual authority that has been given you by faith in Jesus' Name! Today Jesus exposes evil spirits and dispatches them quickly, just as He did when He lived on this earth. The only difference is that now He does this through the people He has called into the ministry of healing.

These are the words one should use when binding and casting out evil spirits: *"In the Name of Jesus Christ and by the power of His cross and blood, I bind you, spirit of (name the spirit), and tell you to leave (name the supplicant) right now, and go directly to Jesus, harming no one on the way."* At the same time the supplicant should also be telling them to leave, using the same deliverance prayer. For instance, if the spirit of fear was harassing the supplicant, then he or she would command it to leave in this way, *"In the Name of Jesus Christ, and by the power of His cross and blood, I bind you, spirit of fear, and tell you to leave me now, and go directly to Jesus, harming no one on the way."*

As you can see, there are several components to this prayer: It is a prayer of command. It is said in the Name of Jesus Christ. As Christians we have the authority to command evil spirits to leave in Jesus' Name. In the Name of Jesus, by the authority of His cross and blood (which are the signs of His triumph over sin and evil), we bind Satan and his minions. We bind them so they cannot pull off any dirty tricks, harassing the deliverance ministers or the supplicant as they leave.

We then tell them to go directly to Jesus. I do not believe in telling evil spirits to go into the pit, or into outer space, or any other place, just to Jesus. Jesus is the One who will render them harmless. It is He who will dispatch them quickly, just as He did when He walked this earth. When this is done, that particular spirit will never be able to harass another person.

Then we command them not to harm anyone else on their way to Jesus. This is important, if spirits are not told this in no uncertain terms, they just may stop along the way and begin to harass another member of our household, someone present at the deliverance, or some defenseless person who happens to get in their way.

Sometimes a deliverance is very difficult and requires a great deal of time and hard work. When this happens, several things may be true: One, there is another traumatic incident, or a series of incidents coming down through the family lines, that needs healing. Ask Jesus what these are. He will show you and quickly bring them to healing. You will know when you have reached the problem that let the harassing spirit into the family lines. When this problem is brought into healing by Jesus, you will be able to bind the spirit and dispatch it quickly, leaving the supplicant with a deep feeling of release.

Two, a curse may have been put on the family lines. As I said before, if a formal curse was put on a family it can only be broken by invoking the name of the Trinity three times. These are the words we use; *"In the name of the Father, Son, and Holy Spirit I break the curse of (name the curse) and make it null and void forever."* Declare this three times and the curse will be broken. Formal curses are invoked in the name of a demonic trinity and only the name of the Holy Trinity has the power to break them.

Because this is a mystery and therefore hard to understand this invocation may sound superstitious. The important thing is not whether we understand it or not, but that it works!

Therefore, if you seem to come to a dead-end and the situation you are praying for does not yield to prayer, stop for a moment. Remember. Jesus is the healer! Focus on Him. Ask Him what is blocking your prayer. If He leads you to believe that there is a curse on the family line, then ask Him to tell you what the name of the curse is. The name of the curse will approximate whatever hurtful behavior you see in the situation you are praying for.

For instance, when praying with a person who had a problem with impotency, I asked Jesus to show us what the root cause was. He took us back into the generations to ancestors who were engaging in bestiality. The supplicant asked Jesus to forgive his ancestors and free his family from the effects of their sinful behavior.

I still had the feeling that our prayer was getting nowhere, so I asked Jesus to let us know what the problem was. He gave us the understanding that a curse of bestiality had been put on the family line a long way back in the generations of the family. This curse had come down through the family line in deviant sexual behaviors, such as adultery and incest. Those who became Christians and resisted the temptation to engage in these practices had problems with impotency.

This man's problem was relieved after we broke the curse by invoking the name of the Holy Trinity three times to make it null and void. Along with that, we felt led to cast out the spirits of bestiality and sexual deviancy that had come in at the time the curse was put on the family. Evil spirits usually tag along with curses and are easily expelled when the curse is broken.

The third problem that may interfere with a deliverance occurs when a person is giving in to the temptation to sin in a way that goes along with the character of the spirit harassing the family line. It is very difficult, if not impossible, to expel that spirit until the supplicant makes a decision not to act in a way that is consistent with its nature.

When the supplicant is able to make this decision, forgiveness must be asked of Jesus for the ways in which he or she has given in to this spirit in the past. After this the supplicant should also ask for forgiveness for the ways in which anyone else in the past and present generations of the family line have given in to the spirit of unforgiveness.

For example, if ancestors did not work their anger through to forgiveness when hurt, spirits of unforgiveness, bitterness, and revenge may have gained control over them and their progeny. These familiar spirits will not leave until the supplicant is able to forgive those who originally hurt his or her ancestors. The supplicant also needs to forgive any person who has hurt anyone in the family since then. Then forgiveness must be sought for any way in which the supplicant may have given in to these revengeful, unforgiving spirits.

If the supplicant has a sincere desire to forgive, the spirits of unforgiveness, bitterness, and revenge will no longer have a hold on the family line. They can then be easily expelled. Jesus will often show many generations of people who came after the original unforgiving ancestor and held on to these spirits because of their own hurts. Patterns like this run through many families. Most of them are caused by old hurts and the spirits that piggybacked on them.

After using the deliverance prayer to evict these evil spirits from their comfortable homes we go back into prayer for the generations, asking Jesus to show us any other hurts or sins that allowed evil spirits to enter. As He shows them to us, we ask Jesus to bring them into healing in the same way. We continue to encourage the supplicant to forgive those in all of the generations of the family who sinned in the same way as the first ancestor, and to ask God's forgiveness for anyway in which he or she has given in to the same sort of sin.

Filling the Void

After delivering a person from evil spirits, it is extremely important to pray for that person to be filled with the Holy Spirit. We ask the Holy Spirit to fill every place in the supplicant that had been occupied by the demons with His power and His love. We also pray that Jesus will send the Holy Spirit back through the generations of the family we have been praying for. Then we ask Jesus to seal the portals of the supplicant's soul and spirit so that the harassing spirits can't get back in.

This soaking with the Holy Spirit is very important. When a deliverance is completed, it is almost as though an empty space is left where the spirits were residing. This space must be filled by the Holy Spirit because the harassing spirits will soon be looking for a way back into their happy home. Only the power of God that comes to us through His Holy Spirit can keep them out.

I hope you understand that this ministry is never undertaken without using the prayers of protection found in Chapter 6. It is also extremely important that the prayer-counselors pray for one another to be washed clean from any spirits that might be clinging to them after each session of generational healing and especially after a deliverance has taken place. A simple prayer binding any spirits that might have attached themselves to you and sending them to Jesus will do. Follow this with a prayer asking Jesus to wash you clean with His living waters and to fill every space within your mind, body, spirit, and soul with the Holy Spirit.

John's Healing

As I have attempted to show, deliverance prayer may take many different forms, depending on the source of the demonization and the needs of the supplicant. With one person it may need to be a direct command, with another the spirits may leave during the Eucharist or during the healing prayer. Sometimes when we feel the supplicant would be upset by hearing us command spirits to leave it has proven effective to say the prayer of command under our breath. When we keep our eyes on Jesus and listen to His directive He shows us just what needs to be done for each person who comes to us.

Jesus is both extremely creative and sensitive. He suits the method to each person's need and it always comes in a way the supplicant will understand. With at least 90% of the people who come for the healing of generations and need deliverance prayer the simplest method is all that is needed. This usually consists of having the person see Jesus taking the spirits out in some way and disposing of them immediately.

An example of the way we do deliverance was the case of a young boy who had been having nightmares after viewing a horror movie. Every night, just as he began to fall asleep, John would see himself taking part in a gruesome murder scene. When his parents found out about this they brought him to me.

From what they described to me, it sounded as though John would need deliverance. I felt very uneasy about doing a deliverance with a person this young. I really underestimated our Lord's creativity and His ability to understand and respond to each person's individual needs.

When John arrived my prayer partner and I went into my study to pray with him. We put him at ease by asking him about his experiences. Then we began to tell him how Jesus brings healing to our inner hurts through prayer. We assured him that Jesus loves us each so much that He always understands and respects our feelings without judging us. Then we went into prayer, asking Jesus to protect us and lead us.

As we did, this John began to see himself in the scenes that were frightening him. We assured him that Jesus was in charge and suggested that he ask Jesus into the scene he was seeing. Immediately Jesus was with him. Jesus stopped the action and showed John that what he was seeing was just a very bad movie which had turned into a nightmare for him because he was so sensitive and vulnerable.

Then Jesus gave John an understanding of the way in which demons piggyback on terrifying experiences in order to gain a foothold in the lives of sensitive young people. He led John to understand that when something frightening or traumatic happens to us, a crack may be made in our spiritual armor and our ancient and defeated enemy, Satan, then sends his troops in and begins to harass and oppress us. He also let John know that He had already defeated these hostile forces.

John felt so much peace in the reassuring presence of Jesus that we almost stopped the prayer session right there. But Jesus' words and an inner uneasiness led us to feel that although the hurt was now healed the oppressing spirits were still there.

My prayer partner led John to expel them in this way: "John, can you see yourself standing in your front yard?" John said, "Yes, I can." She said, "Can you see Jesus standing in front of you?" "Yes." "Now look at your self. Can you see the dark clouds inside of you?" "Yes." "Well, Jesus wants you to pull them out and give them to Him, but first He wants you to name them." John said, "One of them is named *horror*." "Tell the spirit of horror to leave you forever and pull it out of your chest and give it to Jesus."

Then John made a motion of tugging at his chest, as if he were pulling something out and handing it to another person. As he did this, he commanded each spirit to leave him and go to Jesus. My partner and I were also silently telling them to leave.

Then my partner asked him, "What has Jesus done with that spirit?" John said, "He has a garbage bag and He rolled it up and threw it into the garbage bag." She then led him to renounce and give to Jesus the spirits of murder, violence, and fear. Each time he would command the evil spirit to leave and then pull the offensive spirit out of his chest cavity and hand it to Jesus. Jesus would then roll it up into a ball and put it into His garbage bag. What a sense of humor Jesus has! He knew right where those spirits belonged: in the garbage!

Then we laid hands on John and prayed for Jesus to fill all of the places in him where the evil spirits had been with the Holy Spirit, and to seal all of the portals of his soul, so that they would not be able to re-enter. As I have already stated, *it is extremely important to pray for the infilling of the Holy Spirit after doing a deliverance!* We then saw Jesus plant within John the seeds of hope, joy, and peace. Jesus then waved goodby and walked off with the garbage bag over His shoulder. As far as we know, John never had another nightmare!

Since the time that we used this approach first with John, we have used this method in three-quarters of the cases where we have perceived the need for deliverance. Jesus continues to surprise us by the different ways He finds to expel evil spirits. A woman who had been abandoned by her father when she was nine years old saw Jesus pull the spirits of abandonment and rejection out of her. Then He rolled them up in a ball and threw them out of the window. Others have seen Him stamp on them and crush them with His heel!

Keeping the Deliverance

After finishing our prayer-session with John, we gave him some advice on how to 'keep' his healing. It is very important to do this, because those harassing spirits want two things; a warm body to exist in, and victory in their battle to keep people from knowing and serving Jesus Christ. So we always advise people to be on their alert after they have received a deliverance. There may be more harassment. The spirits may try to bother a person who has been delivered of them, in the hopes that this person will then fall back into the old ways of thinking and reacting. When this happens, these spirits have, in effect, been given the signal that its all right for them to come back in.

In order to keep this from happening, we must learn some basic Christian rules of living. We must learn to stand firm on the promises of Jesus Christ, who said He would never leave us or forsake us. Whenever we feel harassed, we must tell these spirits that we belong to Jesus, *"In the name of Jesus Christ, get away from me, spirit of (name the spirit), I will not listen to you any longer. I am a child of God. I belong to Jesus Christ. You cannot harass me any longer. Leave me now and go to Jesus, harming no one on the way."*

A friend once said to me, "Just because the delivery man brings a package to the door with our name on it doesn't mean we have to accept it." We don't have to accept anything that is not from Jesus Christ! However, we do need to fill our minds and spirits with positive thoughts of Him and His loving presence with us.

A good way to do this is to keep reminding ourselves of some of the injunctions St. Paul set forth in his epistles, "Praise the Lord in all circumstances." "Everything works for good for those who love the Lord and are called according to His purposes." "Rejoice in the Lord, again I say rejoice!" God is sovereign over every situation in our lives, if we can't see a reason to rejoice we need to ask Him to show it to us, and He will!

Then we begin to practice good Christian disciplines: Lead a well-disciplined Christian life. Spend time with Jesus every day in prayer and Bible study. Attend church and receive the sacraments as often as possible. Join a support group, such as a Christian study group. Take part in a twelve-step group that meets regularly, such as Alcoholics Anonymous, or some other Christian group based on these programs. If necessary, go to a counselor to find help in learning how to deal with old dysfunctional patterns of living and thinking. Undergo spiritual direction. Find a Christian friend to share with.

As Don Basham writes, "Getting rid of the negatives in our life is but half the struggle: each subtraction must be followed immediately by an addition." [1]

Agnes' Story

In almost every case where the root cause is healed, the harassing spirits leave very easily. However, some people have had so much sin and hurt coming down through the generations, and in their present-day family that they need more help.

A good example of this took place when a woman named Agnes came to me for healing. Agnes was an incest victim. She had come to me several years before for healing of memories. At that time, the Lord had revealed the incidents where she had been molested. As with most incest victims, she needed both healing of memories prayer and psychotherapy. After coming to me for healing of memories for a while, we both decided that she should concentrate on getting the help she needed through counseling.

It was several years later when she came back to me for healing of generations. She was still under the care of a counselor and a psychiatrist. But she had come to a place where she didn't feel she was able to progress any further. She had begun to look into her family history and had seen a pattern of incest coming down through the generations. She now felt she could go no further until she had prayers for healing of that pattern.

We celebrated a Eucharist for Agnes' family line each time she came for healing prayer. Each time the Lord would take us back into the generations to show us an incident that was extremely hurtful. The first session we did with her was the easiest for her to bear and was healed without incident. However, the second session involved brother-sister incest within the generations, and this was much more painful for her.

Jesus led us to believe that the parents of the children we were seeing were royalty, and that they had introduced their children to this practice because this was a way to keep them from becoming involved with the common people who lived around them. Agnes was horrified at this scene. As we asked Jesus into it to heal it, she began to sob, great heaving, wracking sobs.

As she sobbed in my partner's arms, the Lord began to bring into my mind the names of the evil spirits that had come into the family line through the incestuous practices of that past generation. As I was given this discernment, I began to name the spirits and command them to leave Agnes and her family line. Every time I commanded a spirit to leave, Agnes would begin to convulse with a coughing spasm. Then she would shake her head to let me know the spirit had left her. We went on like this for about three-quarters of an hour, expelling one spirit after another. Then she stopped crying and settled back into her chair with a very peaceful look on her face.

The next time she came we had a really difficult problem. As soon as we went into prayer Agnes saw herself down at the bottom of a pit. Flying all around her were gargoyle-like creatures. She was in great fear of them. I asked her where Jesus was. She said He was at the top of the pit looking down. I suggested that she ask Jesus to come down into the pit with her, but she was too afraid. The Lord led us to understand that this was because her own father had been so distant from her. Like a lot of people who come to us, Agnes expected Jesus, as representative of her heavenly Father, to neglect her needs just as her earthly father had.

At this point, we knew we had to stop and heal the childhood hurts that had led to this warped view of God. We did this by having her see herself with her father when she was a small child and then ask Jesus into the scene to heal it. After Jesus healed this childhood memory, He held the baby Agnes in His arms and softly told her He would always be there to protect her. As He told her this, she saw herself back in the pit, but this time Jesus was with her in the corner.

We then asked Jesus what the root cause was that had allowed all of these evil spirits into the family line. He took us back to a time when Agnes' ancestors were involved in pagan worship which had included ritualistic sexual practices. There was a hideous looking man leading this worship. Agnes asked Jesus to bring her ancestors to repentance and forgive them and anyone else in her family line who had given in to these practices. She saw her ancestors kneel down and ask forgiveness of Jesus. However, the leader just backed away into the darkness behind him, seeming to choose the darkness rather than the light that Christ offered him.

When this episode seemed to be healed, Jesus again gave me discernment as to the nature and names of the spirits Agnes had been seeing in the scene in the pit. As He did this, I bound them in His name and commanded them to leave Agnes and her family line. Every time I did this all three of us would see Jesus grab one of the gargoyle-like spirits. Then He would grind it under His foot until it disappeared into nothingness.

There were several spirits that wouldn't leave when commanded to. These seemed to be some that had been in her family line for a long time. They were securely entrenched because those in her present-day family often gave into them. These were the spirits of incest, lies, and mockery. In order to get them to leave we had to do a more formal, or 'eyeball-to-eyeball' type of deliverance.

This means that you have to look directly into the supplicant's eyes and command the spirits to leave, using the words of command. As I looked into Agnes' eyes, I commanded the spirits to leave one at a time. This was quite a struggle, because they had control of Agnes and of others in her family for such a long time.

Sometimes spirits like these will talk back to you, telling you that they will not leave because the person you are working with belongs to them. This is the a lie, because if the person you are working with is a Christian, that person belongs to Jesus Christ!

It took us about three-quarters of an hour to finish this deliverance with Agnes. Then we prayed for her to be filled with the Holy Spirit in all of the places where these evil spirits had been. We then prayed for Jesus to seal all of the portals of her soul and spirit, so that they could not come back in.

After having done this we knew that there was only one way those spirits could come back in, that is, if Agnes allowed them to! A person can let them back in by giving in to the temptation to act in a way that is consistent with the nature of the harassing spirit. Because of this, I always warn the supplicant to strongly resist any such temptation.

However, Agnes was still in need of much healing when she left us and a few hours later she called to ask for more help. I couldn't understand what had happened, as we seemed to have done everything needed. She was staying with a friend because she felt she could no longer be comfortable living with her parents. When her mother had called to ask why she was not coming home Agnes had told her a lie, rather than try to explain the truth. The spirit of lies then had the opening it needed to come back in.

We went back into prayer to expel it. As we did, Agnes began to sob again. She was remembering a time when she had been terribly hurt. This was the hurt that had allowed the spirit of lies to have such a strong hold on her. It was a time when a terrible lie had been perpetrated by a member of her family and, although grievously hurt by it, she had gone along with it in order to keep peace in the family. I advised her to confess it to Jesus and ask His forgiveness for it. As she did this, she again began to cough convulsively, and the spirit of lies left her. We again went through prayers to fill her with the Holy Spirit and close the portals of her soul and spirit. This time Agnes knew that she would have to be vigilant for a long while in order to 'keep' the healing she had fought so hard for.

Most of the time deliverance is very simple when doing healing of generations, as long as the wound that let the spirits enter in the first place has been healed. Agnes' case history shows a variety of ways in which this might be done, but in at least three-quarters of the people I see there is no need to go into a formal deliverance. Most of the deliverance is done very simply, just as we did in John's case history.

Working in Concert with Jesus

Remember, you are a child of God and a co-worker with Jesus Christ as He carries on His plan of freeing His people from Satan's domination. Jesus died upon the cross for our sins. When He did this, His shed blood broke Satan's power for all time. As those who have been ransomed by that blood, we no longer need to be afraid of these harassing spirits. They are subject to the Name of Jesus Christ. We, the members of the Body of Christ, the Church, are those who have been given the privilege to use that Name. When we use the Name of Jesus to cast out evil spirits they shake with fear, because they know they are defeated by it!

The only problem we face is when we are not strongly convicted of this fact. Satan and his minions play mind games with us and try to convince us that they are more powerful than we are. That is not true! The truth is that Jesus Christ our Lord has given His power to us to use as we work in concert with Him to bring His people into healing.

Those whom He calls, He also prepares. If you have been called to this ministry, He will prepare you by giving you the gifts of discernment and faith. You will understand deep within your inner being the nature of the harassment the supplicant is under and, as you gain experience in this ministry, you will also grow in faith.

Your faith can never be founded on your own power or ability, but on the solid knowledge that our Lord Jesus Christ has already defeated Satan and that Jesus' deepest desire is to see His people whole. He will accomplish this through healing of generations, healing of memories, and deliverance prayer as we follow His directions, and His directions only. In this way the hold Satan has on the life of the person we are praying with will be broken.

If you wish to know more about the ministry of deliverance read *Deliverance from Evil Spirits by* Francis McNutt; *Deliver Us From Evil* by Don Basham; or *Deliverance Prayer* by Matthew and Dennis Linn. Another good source is *Deliverance Conference Highlights*, a two-hour video tape put out by Christian Healing Ministries.[2]

Remember that this ministry is not for amateurs. No amount of reading will take the place of the gifts of discernment and faith, and the experience that comes from working with someone who has been called and tested in the ministry of deliverance!

If you encounter a problem that does not yield to the methods I have detailed, do not try to handle it alone. Find a person who is gifted and experienced in deliverance ministry. I am sure that if you need help in helping a person through deliverance, our providential God will be there with just the person who will fill that need. He is Jehovah Jirah, our provider! He doesn't leave His people hurting and in need without providing just the right person to help them!

Chapter Ten

God is Raising an Army!

Then they cried to the Lord in their trouble,
and He saved them from their distress;
He sent out His word and healed them
and saved them from destruction.
Psalm 107:18,19

God is raising an army. He is preparing His people to do battle against all of the forces of darkness that prevail upon this earth. Part of this preparation is to heal the hurts of His people so that they will be freed to serve Him without any hindrance.

The Church has always recognized that Christians were called to be members of an army, doing battle with our ancient enemy, Satan. At my baptism the priest said this prayer over me as he signed my forehead with the sign of the cross of Christ;

We receive this child into the congregation of Christ's flock; and do sign her with the sign of the cross, in token that hereafter she shall not be ashamed to confess the faith of Christ crucified, and manfully to fight under His banner, against sin, the world, and the devil; and to continue Christ's faithful soldier and servant unto her life's end. Amen.[1]

This prayer aptly acknowledges one of the major truths of Christianity, that those who make a decision to follow and serve

Jesus Christ must expect to join in a battle. We do not fight against flesh and blood, but against unseen forces: *sin, the world, and the devil*. To be *Christ's faithful soldier and servant* means to be actively engaged in that battle. It means to acknowledge that these unseen forces never stop in their fight to keep us from receiving the wholeness we need in order to actively serve under our Lord and Savior, and to *continue Christ's faithful soldier and servant until our lives end*.

Healing of generations is only for those who have made a conscious decision to join the battle against the hurt and sin that have kept our families in captivity for generation after generation. We are to be soldiers actively engaged in combat and we must conduct ourselves accordingly. Our preparation for this ministry can be compared to the training a person goes through when joining an army.

First the person makes a decision to join the military force and does so. Second, this person is given equipment to use as a member of this army. Third, he or she is given training in order to learn how to be a good soldier and use the equipment received. Only then does this person actually gain experience as a soldier by going into battle. We will see how this works out in the life of a person who has decided to join the Christian fray by becoming a healing of generations prayer-counselor.

I. Making the Decision to Join God's Army

People may either be drafted for a country's army or they may freely decide to sign up on their own. In this country most people make their own decisions. But there is still a process called 'recruitment', that is, the government publicizes the fact that they have a need for more soldiers and people are urged to join the armed forces.

When it comes to calling people into a ministry within the Body of Christ, God works in a similar way. He lets people know that there is a need. Most of the time He shows us our own need first and then we look around for someone to minister healing to us. As we are healed of our own hurts and our family's past hurts, we learn through the experience how to minister healing of generations to others.

Seek the Lord's Direction

After we have received healing, we may feel that we are being led to minister this type of healing to others. This is the time to seek the Lord's direction, asking Him if He is calling you to work in this ministry. If the answer is a positive feeling that He is, check this out with your pastor or priest. This is a ministry for the local parish church and should always be carried on under the authority of its leader.

If your pastor or priest supports you in this ministry, you should think over the admonishment Jesus gave in these verses from the Gospel of Luke:

> Whoever does not bear his own cross and come after me, cannot be my disciple. For which of you, desiring to build a tower, does not first sit down and count the cost, whether he has enough to complete it?
>
> Luke 14:27,28

This is not a ministry to be taken on without a lot of thought and prayer. It takes time, energy, and commitment. When you do healing of generations you are making a commitment to work until the healing is complete. This is not always easy, so make sure you count the cost. If you still feel called to this ministry, make a definite decision to dedicate yourself to serving Christ and His people as a healing of generations prayer-counselor.

A few years ago I was giving a 10-week course on the healing of generations for the Order of St. Luke in Falmouth, Massachusetts. At that time, I was interim rector of the Church of the Messiah in Wood's Hole, just a few miles outside of Falmouth. Falmouth is on the Atlantic Ocean at the beginning of Cape Cod. I learned throughout that winter that the ocean winds blow hard and cold there.

The course began on an especially frigid, blustery Thursday night in January. I think it was the coldest night I had ever experienced. I was dressed in layer upon layer of warm clothing.

In the class there were three stalwart women from Martha's Vineyard, an island off the coast of Falmouth. On that bitter cold night, their dedication to the healing ministry was so great that they had taken the ferry over to the mainland, even though the temperatures were so low and the wind so high that it must have been at the cost of great discomfort. I was so impressed that I offered to go over to the island to teach their small group of OSL members (but not until the warm spring breezes had come).

Make a firm commitment

Writing to the Philippians Paul said, "Work out your own salvation with fear and trembling." (Philippians 2:12) The word he used for 'salvation' can also be interpreted as wholeness or healing. Those who work in a ministry of healing should take their own needs for healing seriously. Otherwise they will run the risk of being too needy to help those who are coming to them for ministry. So, make a firm commitment to set aside a regular time each week when you will meet with two or more friends and pray for one another for the healing of generations.

The first night of the Falmouth course I suggested that each person there find two friends to work with and that they then agree to meet together at a regular time each week. I still believe that this is the best way to receive your own healing and learn how to minister to others. Nothing beats experience!

The time you set aside for healing prayers with one another has to be time that you know will not interfere with other events or be interfered with by other demands. It is an appointment you are making with the Lord. It must be honored as such. Your church doesn't change the time of its worship service at the whim of its members. You must see this time for healing as just such a sacred contract.

That is not the only reason for meeting regularly each week. There are at least two more. One is our tendency to put things like this off if we haven't made a strong commitment to them. We have an enemy who is both deceiver and accuser (Revelation 12:9,10). He will use our lack of commitment to try to influence us into feeling that our problems aren't important enough to pay attention to, or that other demands are more important. In this way we might end up dismissing our need for healing entirely.

But think of it in this way; what could be more important to our families than for us to receive the wholeness we need? What could be more important to the Lord and to our ministry within the church than to heal and cut off those things which keep us from functioning fully as a member of Christ's Body?

There is another reason to meet weekly. When we begin to do prayers for healing of generations, we are allowing hurts that have been covered over for a very long time to come up into our consciousness in order to be healed. If we don't work on these hurts regularly, as they come up, we run the risk of pushing them down and covering them over again, perhaps forever. The best way to make sure this doesn't happen is to meet together weekly, allocating one hour for each person's healing (although in the beginning this may take longer).

The three women from Martha's Vineyard exemplify this kind of commitment. From the first week of the class until the present time, some four years later, they have continued to meet faithfully every week at the same time. Even before they had finished the course, they were amazed at how much healing they had received just by honoring this injunction to meet weekly.

Our Lord has always been their leader. They enter into prayer and He brings into their minds what they are to pray for. As they follow His lead, He brings their generational hurts into healing. They have received much healing themselves and have been instrumental in bringing many others into generational healing.

II. The Christian Soldier's Equipment

As soon as a new soldier gets to camp, he goes directly to the stock room and receives the equipment he will need to use as a member of the army. As Christian soldiers we also have 'equipment' we can use.

A Relationship with the Triune God

The most important piece of equipment that we can have is a deep faith that comes from a relationship with our triune God: Father, Son, and Holy Spirit.

Let us start with God the Father. So many of us have been hurt by our human fathers that we may not have been able to develop any real trust in our heavenly Father. We may judge God by the way our earthly father behaved toward us.

If our father was abusive, we may think God will always punish us. If our father wasn't there for us when we needed Him, we may think God will leave us just at the moment we need Him the most.

My father died when I was five years old, and even though I didn't realize it until many years later, the child within me always thought her father had abandoned her, and her heavenly Father would abandon her if she didn't do exactly what He asked.

The good news is that God isn't like our earthly fathers! Some fathers may in their best moments come close to being like God, but all are affected in some way by the sin and ambiguity inherent to human nature.

There is no human being, no matter how loving, who is able to love us as God does. God's love is totally unconditional. There is nothing we can ever do that will change His love for us. John wrote, "See what love the Father has given us, that we should be called children of God; and that is what we are." (1 John 3:1)

Only in our most transcendent moments can we experience such deep devotion. This devotion comes not because of what we have done, but just because we exist. We need to know this for our own sake and for the sake of those we minister to. God our Father created us to love, and He loves each and every one of us as though we were the only one ever created. *What wondrous love is this!*

Put on the Lord Jesus Christ

People who wish to minister in Jesus' name should have a personal relationship with Him that results from having made a definite decision to ask Him to be their Savior, and from daily inviting Him to be present in their lives as Lord.

This is elemental. Central to each Christian's life should be his or her relationship with Jesus. Jesus is the healer, we are only tools through whom He works to set His people free. If we do not have a deep personal relationship with Him, how will we be able to let Him use us? How will we be able to teach others to trust Him enough to allow Him into the deeply hurting places in their lives and in the past generations of their family lines?

Even with a deep faith in Jesus, we start out on this journey with great hesitancy. We may trust Him, but we seldom have much faith in His capacity to work through us. We know our weaknesses only too well. As I said before, a common feeling when beginning to pray with a person is, "This person's problems are too difficult. This is the person we won't be able to help." This happens to us so many times, it must be the enemy's greatest lie.

Truly, truly, I say to you, he who believes in me will also do the works that I do; and greater works than these will he do, because I go to the Father. Whatever you ask in my name, I will do it, that the Father may be glorified in the Son; if you ask anything in my name, I will do it.

John 14:12-14

As these verses from John 14 show, Jesus has promised that we will be able to do mighty works when we ask in His Name. In fact He tells us that we will be able to do even greater works than He has done. As we pray for the healing of generations with people, it is important to remember that Jesus is faithful to His promise to do a mighty work through us, so that God may be glorified as people are healed and enabled to worship Him and serve Him.

Empowered by the Holy Spirit

A very important part of the Christian soldier's equipment is the empowerment of the Holy Spirit. Pray for the power of the Holy Spirit to be released in your life and ministry. Ask others to pray for you to be empowered by the Holy Spirit. Ask God to reveal the

Holy Spirit to you as a person with whom you can have an intimate relationship.

We very seldom think of the Holy Spirit as a person whose friendship we should cultivate. Yet Jesus spoke of the Holy Spirit as the Counselor or Advocate, both roles consonant with personhood. In healing of generations prayer we are led by the Holy Spirit, as He guides us and gives us the wisdom and understanding we need to carry on this ministry.

The Gifts of the Spirit

Ask, and it will be given you; seek, and you shall find; knock, and it will be opened to you. For everyone who asks receives, and he who seeks finds, and to him who knocks it will be opened. Or what man of you, if his son asks him for a loaf, will give him a stone? Or if he asks for a fish, will give him a serpent? If you them, who are evil, know how to give good gifts to your children, how much more will your Father who is in heaven give good things to those who ask him?
Matthew 7:7-11

One of the most important things we can do each day is to pray for the spiritual gifts of compassion, faith, and discernment that we need for carrying on this ministry for the Lord. If we couple the above verses from Matthew 7 with the verses from John 14:13,14 where Jesus says, "Whatever you ask in my name, I will do it, that the Father may be glorified in the Son; if you ask anything in my name, I will do it," we will begin to see how strongly Jesus desires to gift us with the ability to serve Him in power.

When Jesus said, "In my name," He meant "according to my character," or "in accordance with my will." It is in accord with His character and will that we ask Him for the gifts we need to bring others into healing, since one third of His ministry while He was on this earth had to do with healing. When we ask for the gifts to carry on this ministry He will graciously give them to us.

However, we may not know He has given them to us until we begin to use them. I remember very clearly, in the early days of my ministry, asking Him over and over for the gift of discernment and the wisdom to know how to use it. One day as I was eagerly praying for them once again, I felt very strongly that God was saying to me, "I have already given you those gifts. When are you going to use them?"

Ouch! I am sure it is the same with any of the gifts, we don't know we have them until we use them. So, pray for the gifts and then step out in faith and begin to use them.

A Compassionate Heart

The one thing the people who come to you will need the most is someone who will understand their pain and be willing to enter into it with them. So, the first gift we ask Jesus to give us is a compassionate heart, so that we will be able to love each person we are praying for with His unconditional, nonjudgmental love.

As we ask Jesus to give us the love He has for each person we work with, He will be faithful to do this. We will find our hearts filled with an understanding of their hurts that we could never attain on our own. We will be able to help them without judging them as Jesus gives us an understanding of why people acted in the way that they did.

I once took a course on compassion with Henri Nouwen. He taught us that at the heart of compassion was a dedication to being 'simply present' with each person we encountered throughout our day. He taught us to be 'self-forgetful', to become so present to the other person that we were able to totally forget our own being and our own needs for the time that we were with him or her.

In *Out of Solitude* Fr. Nouwen writes:

> Every human being has a great, yet often unknown, gift to care, to be compassionate, to become present to the other, to listen, to hear and to receive. If that gift would be set free and made available, miracles could take place. Those who really can receive bread from a stranger and smile in gratitude, can feed many without even realizing it. Those who can sit in silence with their fellowman not knowing what to say but knowing that they should be there, can bring new life in a dying heart. Those who are not afraid to hold a hand in gratitude, to shed tears in grief, and to let a sigh of distress arise from the heart, can break through paralyzing boundaries and witness the birth of a new relationship, the fellowship of the broken.[2]

As you can see from this quotation, to be compassionate means to be able to suffer with another person, to be able to put yourself in the other's shoes and feel the pain he or she is experiencing. Only as you are able to feel another person's pain, and still trust in God's desire and power to heal that person, will you be able to help that person to encounter Christ and thus find healing for the painful places in his or her life.

Faith

Pray for a firm faith in Jesus Christ, our Lord. The writer of the Letter to the Hebrews tells us that "faith is the assurance of things hoped for, the conviction of things not seen." (Hebrews 11:1)

Just as this writer uses Abraham as an example of one who "obeyed when he was called to go out . . . not knowing where he was to go" (Hebrew 11:8), so we, too, are called by God to step out in faith, especially when we don't really know how we are going to be able to help the person we are praying for. As we do this, Jesus will use us to bring our brothers and sisters into wholeness, because He is always there to meet and heal a person who comes to Him for help.

Our faith is never in ourselves or whatever ability we may have. It is always in our Lord Jesus Christ, in His power and deep desire to bring all of humankind into wholeness and healing. If you ever doubt Jesus' deep desire to heal all who come to Him for help, just think of the way in which He gave His life for us. In His sacrificial death upon the cross, Jesus gave Himself up to pain and agony. He did this so that we could be freed from our sins and reunited once again with His Father. Through His resurrection, Jesus showed us that He had been given power over death and the grave. Meditating on Jesus' death and resurrection always infuses me with a strong faith in the depth of His love for us, and in His deep desire to heal each person who comes to Him in faith.

Remember what took place just after Jesus came down from the Mount of Transfiguration? There was a man whose son had a spirit that threw him into the fire and tried to kill him. He wanted to see his son healed. He had some faith in Jesus, but he didn't feel that his faith was strong enough. His words were, "I believe, help my unbelief!" Even this trembling faith was enough, for Jesus healed his son completely.

There are times when every one of us feels like that man. We may have faith, but there is also an element of doubt that creeps in. It is not so much doubt in Jesus' ability or desire to give healing to the person we are praying with, as it is doubt in our ability to be the proper vehicle for that healing. We feel that Jesus will not use us to bring others into healing because we know our own humanity, our own sinfulness, too well. We sometimes feel as though our spiritual 'ozone layer' is depleted, just as the atmospheric one is, and we can't get past the weight of a sinful world that breaks in upon us.

Thankfully, God's ability to use us doesn't depend on any state of perfection we might be able to attain, or on our momentary feelings, but only on the grace of our loving Father. This is so true that I would like to repeat it over and over again: When we go to

God for help, He is always there to meet us, no matter what our present state is. When a person comes to me for prayer, I know they did not come because of whom I am, or what I can do for them. They come to me because they want to meet God. They want His love and His healing in their lives. *Therefore, He is always there to meet them and to fill their needs. Despite us! Despite our sinfulness! Despite our ineptitude! God can and will help anyone who sincerely desires to be healed, as long as they are willing to go through the hard work involved.*

Discernment

When the Spirit of truth comes, He will guide you into all the truth; for He will not speak on His own authority, but whatever He hears He will speak
. . .

John 16:18

A soldier must learn to hear and obey each order his commander-in-chief gives before acting upon it. We, too, must be able to understand how God wants us to proceed in each situation. God gives us this understanding through the gift of discernment. When I use this term, I am speaking of the ability to listen deeply and responsively to both God and the person who comes for healing prayer. This gets to be a kind of juggling act, as we learn to listen to God with one ear, while listening to the supplicant with the other.

My first attempts to be a good listener weren't too successful. My mind wandered. It went off in a hundred different directions. I was the last person in the world that anyone would ever think could help people by being totally with them. So I learned that listening is not easy. Our minds are too full of our own agenda. We carry too many voices from the past within us and maybe too much pressure from the present. But listening may just be one of the most important parts of our ministries.

I have found that I cannot truly listen to another human being in any real depth unless I have spent time each day in silence with God. The outcome of this time in silence is the ability to know, at a very deep level, how God is leading me.

I also need to have a friend who can listen to me, someone who can bear to hear my problems and complaints, anxieties and sorrows, triumphs and joys, and not be overwhelmed by them, someone who will help me to concentrate on God and His ability to fill my every need. This I receive through loving Christian friends and through the aid of a spiritual director.

There may be others who are more gifted in this area who wouldn't need this, but I do. And I have come to a point where I can accept my own needs as valid. So I regularly meet with a friend who listens to me, so that I can empty myself of the inner voices and hear the stories others wish to share with me.

III. Basic Training

After they have received their equipment, soldiers begin to receive training, both physical and mental, in army discipline and action. As Christian soldiers we also need to receive instruction in discipline and action. However, since our battle is a spiritual one, we need to learn spiritual disciplines in order to serve our Lord well.

Bible Study

Blessed Lord, who caused all holy Scriptures to be written for our learning: Grant us so to hear them, read, mark, learn, and inwardly digest them, that we may embrace and ever hold fast the blessed hope of everlasting life, which you have given us in our Savior Jesus Christ; who lives and reigns with you and the Holy Spirit, one God, forever and ever. Amen.[3]

This collect aptly describes why Scripture was written: "for our learning . . . that we may embrace and ever hold fast the blessed hope of everlasting life." So first and foremost, we study the Bible and practice all spiritual disciplines for our own sake, so that we will come to know our Lord Jesus Christ, and the sweetness of His love. Only after this is accomplished do we use these disciplines as a basis for helping others to receive the healing and wholeness that Jesus offers.

A good knowledge of Scripture is basic for anyone wanting to become a prayer-counselor. The kind of knowledge needed comes very easily through reading and meditating on Bible passages daily. I suggest reading a passage a day, asking three questions about it: What did this passage mean to those who first heard it in Jesus' day? What does it mean to us today? How does God want me to apply this to my own life?

When I first began praying with people, I felt I should have a good familiarity with Scripture. I wanted to be able to put into a person's hands just the verse that would meet each particular need. I really was afraid I would never be able to do this. I had never been able to memorize well. I kept on reading and studying the Bible daily, using the Daily Office Lectionary from the Book of Common Prayer. I applied these three questions to everything I read, but I did not really attempt to memorize verses.

As I did this, I found out that even though I was not memorizing it verse by verse, the truth of this sacred book was there for me when I needed it. I would be praying with a person and just the right verse of Scripture would pop into my mind as soon as I needed it. This was just another sign of the wonderful graciousness of our God. My need for direction and edification was met as I studied, and the Lord also used my study to make me aware of passages that would help to bring wholeness to those I ministered to.

Prayer

In the morning, a great while before day, He rose and went out to a lonely place, and there He prayed. And Simon and those who were with Him pursued Him, and they found Him and said to Him, "Everyone is searching for you." And He said to them, "Let us go on to the next towns, that I may preach there also; for that is why I came out."

Mark 1:35-38

I've already spoken of the need to spend time alone with God in Bible study and prayer. Now let's think about the content of that time. As with many people who have a healing ministry, my first call was to serve God as an intercessor. Intercessory prayer has always been a strong part of my prayer life. However, intercessions should be only one part of our daily prayer regime. Added to this should be time meditating on Bible passages, time in quiet enjoying the Lord's presence, and time in worship and adoration.

We hear a lot of talk today about the difference between quality time and quantity of time. My feeling is that we need to give God both quality time and quantity of time. I've never thought that I was able to get much quality out of just a few minutes of prayer each day. I know definitely that the quality of my life changes as I give Him, not just the best part of my day, but a good amount of my time as well.

I have found that I have to spend at least an hour alone with Him each day in order for my life to be guided and supported by Him, and in order to be able to minister to others in and with His love.

I also understand that each person's situation is different, and that there are others who serve Him well without being able to give Him this amount of time.

So I am sure that in His wonderful economy God will accomplish His purposes through these people as long as they truly give Him as much time as they can and really desire to know Him, worship Him, and serve Him. But I also know that He longs to have His people seek Him out for quiet communion, and that our lives are lesser for the want of that gifted time.

The Gospels show us that even Jesus needed time alone with His Father. In Mark's Gospel we see that Jesus 'went out to a lonely place' and prayed before making decisions about how to carry on His ministry. We need to follow Him into this place of solitude and communion, which will lead us into ministry and new life. Henri Nouwen writes,

> In solitude we can listen to the voice of him who spoke to us before we could speak a word, who healed us before we could make any gesture to help, who set us free long before we could free others, and who loved us long before we could give love to anyone. It is in this solitude that we discover that being is more important than having, and that we are worth more than the result of our efforts. In solitude we discover that our life is not a possession to be defended, but a gift to be shared. It's there we recognize that the healing words we speak are not just our own, but are given to us; that the love we can express is part of a greater love; and that the new life we bring forth is not a property to cling to, but a gift to be received.[4]

There are many ways to use this time with God. For many years I have begun my own time of solitude and prayer with the office of Morning Prayer from the Book of Common Prayer. This ancient, formal prayer office has been invaluable to me. It has kept me going through times when I have felt lost in a desert wasteland to times when I have been able to praise the Lord with all that is in me.

Because I have kept faithful to this as a spiritual discipline, the Lord has faithfully used it to call me to Him, even when I have been in the pit of despair. Prayer is a discipline, but it is also a way to walk with a Friend. This Friend is often difficult to know, especially when we are living in the midst of a dark and pain-filled world. The use of some kind of formal prayer guide helps us to find our way when the way gets rough.

In the office of Morning Prayer, lessons from the Daily Office Lectionary are interspersed with psalms and canticles of praise. Confession and Apostles Creed keep our spiritual life on course. Prayers and intercessions round it out. Some people might find this type of prayer too formal. But I find it the perfect springboard to deep communion with our Lord.

After doing the daily office I spend time in the practice of silent prayer, sometimes called contemplative or centering prayer. I quiet my inner being by just sitting in Jesus' presence until I feel His gaze upon me.

I free my mind of all thought and softly say His name over and over again deep within my inner being. I have learned that repetition slows my mind down so that I am able to let go of any thoughts and images that come into my mind.

I may repeat a verse from the Psalms: "For God alone my soul in silence waits." (Psalm 62:1) I may use the Jesus Prayer, "Lord Jesus Christ, Son of the living God, have mercy upon me, a sinner." But most of the time I just repeat our Lord's name, 'Jesus', softly within myself. I say it just long enough to quiet down and feel myself in His presence.

If you are interested in this type of prayer, I would suggest reading *Experiencing the Depths of Jesus Christ* by Madame Jeanne Guyon. Mme. Guyon writes, " . . . we have all been called to the depths of Christ just as surely as we have been called to salvation." She goes on to say that having a " . . . deep, inward relationship to Jesus Christ . . . " involves " . . . only the turning and yielding of your heart to the Lord."[5] Her words on the life of prayer draw one quickly into the presence of Christ.

When we are in silent prayer thoughts and images will appear in our consciousness. When this happens just allow them to float by like a boat on the gentle current of a river. There is nothing so important as being with Jesus. Trust Him with your time and with your life. There is nothing that comes into your mind that cannot wait until your time of communion with Jesus is over.

It is important to remember that there is no such thing as success or failure in prayer. As long as you give this time to the Lord, He will bless you. You will begin to feel the joy and peace of His presence in your life in a much deeper way. You will be able to minister to others out of the strength of Christ, as you remain more centered on Him than on your own problems or theirs.

Participation in the Body of Christ

If I look at myself, I am nothing. But if I look at us all I am hopeful; for I see the unity of love among all my fellow-Christians. In this unity lies our salvation.

Julian of Norwich

An essential part of any Christian discipline must be participation in the life of the Church, the Body of Christ. This is elemental to one who wishes to carry on a ministry of Christian healing. Each one of us needs the support, nurturing, inner strength, and discipline that comes from belonging to and worshiping regularly with a local Christian parish. We need to be strengthened by the sacrament of Holy Communion (Lord's Supper, Mass). We need to be disciplined by the sacrament of reconciliation (confession). We need the prayerful and loving support of Christian friends, who will be interceding for us as we carry on this ministry, and with whom we can candidly speak of our needs and still be understood and loved.

It is also helpful for us to be working with a spiritual director who will offer to us understanding, direction, and a steadying influence. This ministry is not an easy one, and we all need help keeping on the right course.

As we take part in this life of discipline and worship, we also take part in the mystical union of all Christian believers with our Lord Jesus Christ, and " . . . complete what is lacking in Christ's afflictions for the sake of his body, that is, the church . . . " (Colossians 1:24). And in our ministry, and in our obedience to Christ and to His Church, we become signs and symbols of His resurrected life, lived out in compassion and servanthood among His followers.

Within the total human community, there is a community which alone is capable of grasping our transcendent vocation. This is the church, a chosen community, whose members are not chosen for privilege but for duty. Christ told us he was sending us out as sheep among wolves. He ordered us to go. On the eve of his resurrection he told us that as his Father had sent him, he sent us. He told us we were like a heavenly colony on earth, an avant-garde of the kingdom of God, fellow soldiers with the Lord in the battle to free the world from the powers of evil and death.[7]

Epilogue

Now he was teaching in one of the synagogues on the sabbath. And just then there appeared a woman with a spirit that had crippled her for eighteen years. She was bent over and was quite unable to stand up straight. When Jesus saw her, he called her over and said, "Woman, you are set free from your ailment." When he laid his hands on her, immediately she stood up straight and began praising God. But the leader of the synagogue, indignant because Jesus had cured on the sabbath, kept saying to the crowd, "There are six days on which work ought to be done; come on those days and be cured, and not on the sabbath day." But the Lord answered him and said, "You hypocrites! Does not each of you on the sabbath untie his ox or his donkey from the manger, and lead it away to give it water? And ought not this woman, a daughter of Abraham whom Satan bound for eighteen long years, be set free from this bondage on the sabbath day?" When he said this, all his opponents were put to shame; and the entire crowd was rejoicing at all the wonderful things that he was doing.

Luke 13:11-17 (NRSV)

Here is a meditation a friend sent me based on these verses from Luke:

We are all like the woman who was bent over for eighteen years. We are bowing, stumbling, not able to "see" heavenward, oppressed by the sins of our forebears. We are bound by Satan through generational sin and bondage.

Jesus healed that woman on the sabbath. He did a new thing. He "went against" the traditionalists. Healing of Generations goes against tradition also. But it is, to date, our most powerful tool to "unbind" us from the oppression of the evil one.

We will experience resistance, because it goes against tradition - and we will be attacked by the spirits of doubt, fear, etc. But we *must* do this work, share this gift of our Lord with those he sends us. This is an extremely valuable seed to be planted and tended. We must be faithful gardeners! It will help to keep the image of this woman in mind, as well as Jesus' response to the "traditionalists" as we do this work.

Laborers into His Harvest

Then he said to his disciples, "The harvest is plentiful, but the laborers are few; pray therefore the Lord of the harvest to send out laborers into his harvest."

Matthew 9:37.38

The subtitle of this book is *A Manual for Ministry*. Webster's Dictionary describes a manual as *"a handy book for use as a guide or reference."* I have written this book to be *used as a guide* for those who wish to carry on a ministry of generational healing. It will be *useless* if it is read and then put back on the bookshelf to gather dust.

This is a demanding ministry, but it is also an exciting and fulfilling ministry. Those whom Christ calls, He also empowers, and those whom He empowers, He also blesses! If you answer His call to minister in this way Jesus Himself will bless you with all of the gifts necessary to carry on this ministry! But, we never know the blessedness of this ministry or any other, if we do not make a decision to carry it on and begin to pray with people for healing of generations.

Almost every person who is now active in this ministry began without any help except for the guidance of the Holy Spirit. It was only as we began to pray with a person that we were led from one hurting incident to another. It was only as we entered into those incidents, fearfully, hesitatingly, with our Lord as guide, that we began to learn. Leaning totally on Him for direction, we began to see people healed of terrible hurts. We were always sinfully aware of our own lack of knowledge and experience. But if we had stopped because of that lack, those people would never have been healed, and we would never have received the experience we needed.

What I am trying to say is this: No one is going to feel completely at home with this or any other ministry until they step out in faith and begin to *just do it*!

Experience, knowledge, and strength come as a by-product of carrying on a ministry. They do not come to us as we wait and wonder about whether we should do it or not!

We are like the proverbial beach-goer who sticks her foot into the water and finding it cold, leaves without the joy of a good swim. Our Lord stands by, watching and shaking His head, *"If only my child had jumped right in, she would have forgotten the coolness of the water for the joy and invigoration of the swim!"*

I cannot urge you strongly enough to get into the swim! Find some friends to work with you and begin to pray for the healing of your own family line and theirs.

The Lord of the harvest is calling you!

From Generation to Generation

Appendix A ~ Genogram

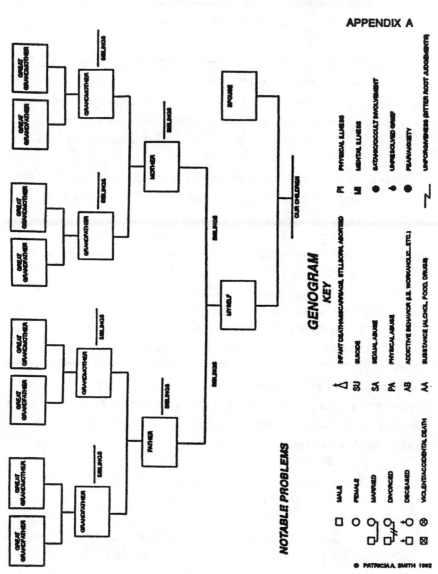

199

Appendix B

The Renunciation of Occult Involvement and the Reaffirmation of Baptismal Vows

There shall not be found among you anyone who burns his son or daughter as an offering, anyone who practices divination, a soothsayer, or an auger, or a sorcerer, or a charmer, or a medium, or a wizard, or a necromancer. For whoever does these things is an abomination to the Lord . .

.Deuteronomy 18:10-12

This is a list of occult, satanic, pagan, and new age practices that hinder healing. They have in common a search for knowledge and power that should belong to God alone. As Christians we are to depend on the gifts of the Holy Spirit given at baptism for the knowledge and power we need. Each time we turn to other sources we turn away from the Lord God Almighty and, in so doing, refuse to wait for the strengthening, uplifting power of the Holy Spirit to fulfil our needs. None of us have any way of knowing how many of our ancestors took part in these things. Therefore, we renounce them for ourselves *and* for those in past generations.

In the Name of Jesus Christ I renounce any and all satanic, occult, pagan or new age practices that I or any other member of my family line, past or present, may have engaged in. This includes, but is not limited to, the following things:

amulets/fetishes/talismans
astral projection
astrology
auras
black magic/white magic
channeling
Christian Science
clairvoyance
contacting the dead

crystals/crystal gazing
cults
demonology
divination of any kind
dungeons and dragons
extrasensory perception
fortune telling
I-ching
idolatry of any form

incantations
levitation
Masonic Order
mediums
mesmerizing
Mormonism
ouija boards
pagan religions
palm reading
pantheism/nature worship
pendulums
pornography
psychic phenomena
pyramids
reincarnation/rebirthing

rosicrucianism
runes/occult writing
Santeria
satanic worship
spiritism
spiritualism
tarot cards
telepathy
thought transfer
transcendental meditation
voodoo practices/worship
witchcraft
worship of the dead
any other occult, pagan,
satanic, or new age practices

I ask Jesus Christ to forgive me, my family members, and my ancestors for turning from Him to these evil imitations of His knowledge and power. I send my forgiveness to any person in my family line who has indulged in these or other sinful practices. I ask Jesus to heal my ancestors, myself, and my family members of any harm these practices may have done.

In a reaffirmation of my baptismal vows:

> I renounce Satan and all the spiritual forces of wickedness that rebel against God.
> I renounce the evil powers of this world which corrupt and destroy the creatures of God.
> I renounce all sinful desires that draw me from the love of God.
> I turn to Jesus Christ and accept Him as my Savior.
> I put my whole trust in His grace and love.
> I promise to follow and obey him as my Lord. Amen.

Appendix C

Scriptural Foundations
for
Generational Prayers

Q. Why do we pray for the dead?

A. We pray for them, because we still hold them in our love, and because we trust that in God's presence those who have chosen to serve him will grow in his love, until they see him as he is.[1]

Prayer for past generations has always been part of the Judeo-Christian tradition. Starting in the Old Testament, we read of Ezra's prayers for the forgiveness of the sins of the present generation and the sins of the "fathers" (those in past generations). Ezra confesses the Israelite nation's sins from its beginnings to the Babylonian captivity, and then enters into a penitential covenant with God. Especially note Nehemiah 9:2:

And the Isrealites separated themselves from all foreigners, and stood and confessed their sins and the iniquities of their fathers.

Perhaps the strongest evidence for the legitimacy of ancestral prayer is from the book of Daniel. Here Daniel identifies himself with the entire nation of Israel, past and present:

"While I was speaking and praying, confessing my sin and the sin of my people Israel . . ."

Daniel 9:20

Making no excuses for the apostasy of the nation, Daniel yet pleads for God's forgiveness:

> I prayed to the Lord my God and made confession, saying: O Lord, the great and terrible God, who keepest covenant and steadfast love with those who love him and keep his commandments, we have sinned and done wrong and acted wickedly and rebelled, turning aside from thy commandments and ordinances; we have not listened to thy servants the prophets, who spoke in thy name to our kings, our princes, and our fathers, and to all the people of the land . . . To us, O Lord, belongs confusion of face, to our kings, to our princes, and to our fathers, because we have sinned against thee.
>
> Daniel 9:4-6,8

In 2 Maccabees a sin offering is taken and prayer said for those fallen in battle who had broken the law by wearing amulets depicting a pagan deity:

> ...and they turned to prayer, beseeching that the sin which had been committed might be wholly blotted out . . . He also took up a collection, man by man, to the amount of two thousand drachmas of silver, and sent it to Jerusalem to provide for a sin offering. In doing this he acted very well and honorably, taking account of the resurrection. For if he were not expecting that those who had fallen would rise again, it would have been superfluous and foolish to pray for the dead. But if he was looking to the splendid reward that is laid up for those who fall asleep in godliness, it was a holy and pious thought. Therefore he made atonement for the dead, that they might be delivered from their sin.
>
> 2 Maccabees 12:42-45

These three passages, each coming at critical points in Israel's history, show that there was a longstanding custom of praying for the deceased members of the community.

When we pray in this way we are depending, as Ezra, Daniel, and Judas Maccabeas did, on the mercies of God who is:

...a God ready to forgive, gracious and merciful, slow to anger, and · abounding in steadfast love . . .

Nehemiah 9:17b

The Communion of Saints

The communion of saints is the whole family of God, the living and the dead, those whom we love and those whom we hurt, bound together in Christ by sacrament, prayer, and praise.[2]

When the New Testament documents were written there was already a strong tradition in place of praying for the deceased members of the community, as these verses from 1 Corinthians show:

Otherwise, what do people mean by being baptized on behalf of the dead? If the dead are not raised at all, why are people baptized on their behalf?

I Corinthians 15:29

Christians have never been sure of how to understand this passage. Do they refer to a practice of being baptized in proxy for catechumenates who had died before undergoing baptism? Were newly converted Christians worried about their family members and friends who died before having a chance to hear about the salvation offered through Jesus Christ?

We really can't know the answer for sure, but the practice does show a vigorous belief in the continuity of Christian life and growth after death. This is in keeping with the Christian belief in the communion of saints. Consistent with this, the author of 2 Timothy 1:18 mentions praying for Onesiphorus after his death.

We also know that a strong belief in praying for the deceased was in place by the time of the Church Fathers. Their faith and their experience combined to tell them that their Savior would never cease seeking those who were in need of salvation.

> . . .the Savior Himself will go forth to meet and welcome the truly repentant. Then, holding forth the shadowless, ceaseless light, the Savior will conduct them into the very presence of His Father, into eternal life, into the kingdom of heaven.
>
> Clement of Alexandria

These early Christian apologists and martyrs wrote of having memorial celebrations of the Eucharist held on the anniversary of a Christian's death. These celebrations generally took place at the grave site of the saint who had gone on to glory.

These practices, along with the above verses from the Old Testament, the Apocrypha, and the New Testament, show us that praying for the deceased was a Jewish custom that continued to be the practice of the followers of Christ.

> For He said, 'I am the God of Abraham, and the God of Isaac, and the God of Jacob.' He is not God of the dead, He is God of the living.
>
> Matthew 22:31,32

Setting the Captives Free

The belief that the deceased could actually grow in grace and favor with God was strengthened by the conviction held by the early church - that during the three days that Jesus' body lay in the tomb before the resurrection He descended to the place of the dead, to preach to "the spirits in prison"- as stated in the Apostles' Creed:

He suffered under Pontius Pilate,
   was crucified, died, and was buried.
He descended to the dead.
   On the third day he rose again.[3]

This belief was undergirded by two passages in the First Letter of
Peter and one in the Epistle to the Ephesians:

> For Christ also died for sins once for all, the righteous for the unrighteous,
> that he might bring us to God, being put to death in the flesh but made
> alive in the spirit; in which he went and preached to the spirits in prison,
> who formerly did not obey, when God's patience waited in the days of
> Noah, during the building of the ark, in which a few, that is, eight persons,
> were saved through water.
>
> 1 Peter 3:18-20

Peter uses the unrighteous people who would not listen to Noah's
message as an example of extreme disobedience. These people
scorned the message God sent through Noah - that their lives would
be lost unless they repented and accepted the method of salvation
God was offering them. Because of this, they perished in the flood.

Now, Peter is saying, even these great sinners, who died centuries
before Jesus came, were given the chance to hear the gospel
message:

> For this is why the gospel was preached even to the dead, that though
> judged in the flesh like men, they might live in the spirit like God.
>
> 1 Peter 4:6

Peter emphasizes the fact that no place was too far for God's
redemptive arm to reach. The Interpreter's Bible Commentary has
this to say about these verses:

> For Peter this dramatic historic event was of utmost significance. It spoke
> of the patience of God. It proclaimed the shame of man's
> procrastination and the folly of his failure to heed the warning of God's

prophet. But even more, it revealed the scope and sweep of the eternal Christ's dominion over the living and the dead of all ages, and the inescapable kingship of him who was dead but is alive forevermore (Rev. 1:18).

In short, at the darkest point in human resistance to God, Christ the victorious Lord was preached, indicating that his victory was not his alone, but one that penetrated even to the realm of the most disobedient dead. (See also John 5:25-29; 8:56; Matt. 27:52.) It is rather the vast range of Christ's descent and ascent that are here accentuated . . . The whole passage is an illustration of a practical truth. He is indicating how Christ in his suffering death is not taken captive but is victor through the Spirit; has indeed taken "captivity captive" and manifested his triumph not only in our world, but in that world which is beyond our world.

... If we ask what value this tradition has for us today, the answer is that wherever men are, Christ has power to save.*

Every Knee Shall Bend, Every Tongue Confess

The power of Christ to save, that extends even beyond the grave, is also spoken of in Ephesians:

> Therefore it is said,
>   "When he ascended on high he
>   made captivity itself a captive,
>   he gave gifts to his people."
> (When it says, "He ascended," what does it mean but that he had also descended into the lower parts of the earth? He who descended is the same one who ascended far above all the heavens, so that he might fill all things.)
>
> Ephesians 4:8-10 (NRSV)

The writer of this passage has a strong faith in the divine rule of Christ. To him, Jesus is King of kings and Lord of lords, now

ascended far above all the heavens, that he might fill all things.
These words bring to mind the powerful picture shown in the 19th
chapter of the Revelation to John. With strong images the writer
portrays Jesus as the righteous warrior, called "Faithful and True,"
who wears "a robe dipped in blood" and "judges and makes war."

> From his mouth issues a sharp sword with which to smite the nations, and
> he will rule them with a rod of iron; he will tread the wine press of the fury
> of the wrath of God the Almighty. On his robe and on his thigh he has a
> name inscribed, King of kings and Lord of lords.
>
> Revelation 19:15-16

Jesus is the Christ, the King of kings and Lord of lords. He is the
great warrior upon the white horse, who leads the armies of God in
righteous fury against the unbelief and apostasy of a world that has
long forsaken the purity and obedience that God demands. *He is
Lord of all!*

His righteousness demands an equal righteousness from His
followers. A righteousness that only He can give. It is a free gift,
offered to all who turn to Him in humility and penitence. It is pure
grace. It does not come as a result of our actions, or as something
we can earn. It comes as each person recognizes Jesus Christ as the
Son of God, and makes a true and faithful commitment to Him as
Lord of all. This is the substance of our faith, and it will never
change.

However, Jesus Christ is also the "crucified One," the "Lamb who
was slain." He is the one who died for us that we might have eternal
life. He is the one who now stands at God's right hand and
intercedes for us. He is the one who guides us, watches over us, and
loves us into wholeness and healing. It is said that each person is as
precious to Him as if each one were the only one ever born! Would
He then stop loving and seeking the person who had not heard or
understood the Gospel message?

If Jesus Christ, the Son of God, cared enough to descend to our
sin-stained earth and be "found in human form", then certainly we

210 From Generation to Generation

can believe that He cared enough to go even further, even into the realm of the dead, to offer eternal life to those imprisoned souls who had never had a chance to hear the Gospel. This is not inconsistent with the miraculous, mysterious nature of the entire salvation event.

Some of the people Jesus leads us to pray for died long before the coming of Christ. They never had a chance to believe in Him and repent of their sins in their own lifetimes. Some of those we pray for were terribly wounded people. Perhaps the pain they bore became like walls that kept them from understanding that the message of salvation was meant for them. They may have been held captive by the suffering and anguish in their own lives, *and* that which came down through the generations of their family lines. God is not vindictive. Indeed, from the beginning of time, His purpose has always been to set people free. The end result of God's great plan to set the captives free may be clearly seen in these verses from Philippians, which proclaim the faith of the early church in His absolute rule over *all* things:

> Therefore God has highly exalted him and bestowed on him the name which is above every name, that at the name of Jesus every knee should bow, in heaven and on earth and under the earth, and every tongue confess that Jesus Christ is Lord, to the glory of God the Father.
>
> Philippians 2:5-11

This anthem states that *every knee will bow, in heaven and on earth and under the earth*! Could this mean that every person who has ever lived will someday clearly hear the Gospel preached and, in full understanding of who Jesus Christ is, have the chance to either turn to Him in repentance and belief, or turn away from Him in desperate, unyielding rebellion?

Truly, truly, I say to you, the hour is coming, and now is, when the dead will hear the voice of the Son of God, and those who hear will live. For as the Father has life in himself, so he has granted the Son also to have life in himself, and has given him authority to execute judgment, because he is the Son of man. Do not marvel at this; for the hour is coming when all who are in the tombs will hear his voice and come forth, those who have done good, to the resurrection of life, and those who have done evil, to the resurrection of judgment.

John 5:25-19

Appendix D

Notes

One: An Ancient Connection

1. Robert G. Hewitt, *Benediction, (The Living Church*, Volume 197, 1988), p. 18.

Two: Preparing the Soil

1. *The Hymnal 1982,* Hymn # 689: **I Sought the Lord**, (New York: The Church Hymnal Corporation, 1985).

Three: Betty's Story

1. *The Book of Common Prayer*, pp. 302, 303.

Four: Root Causes of Present-Day Problems

1. Everett L. Fullam, *How to Walk with God*, (Nashville: Oliver-Nelson Books, 1987), p. 23.
2. Alan Richardson, **A Theological Word Book of the Bible**, (London: Camelot Press Ltd., 1950), p. 156.
3. Phoebe Cranor, *Jesus Heals Our Childhood Vows*, (Pecos: Dove Publications, 1966).
4. Dr. Kenneth McAll, *Healing the Family Tree*, (London: Sheldon Press, 1982), pp. 6,7.

5. ibid, p. 7.
6. ibid, p. 19.
7. ibid, p. 49.

Five: The Power of Intercessory Prayer

1. Paul Yongi Cho, *Prayer: Key to Revival*, (Dallas: Word Publishing, 1984), p. 85.
2. Anthony Bloom and Georges LeFebvres, *Courage to Pray*, (New York: Paulist Press, 1973), p. 54.
3. Dick Eastman, *The Hour That Changes the World*, (Grand Rapids: Baker Book House, 1978), p. 78.

Six: Steps to Healing of Generations

1. Everett L. Fullam, *How to Walk With God*, (Nashville: Oliver-Nelson Books, 1987), p. 19.

Eight: The Healing Power of the Holy Eucharist

1. Charles P. Price and Louis Weil, *Liturgy for Living*, (New York: The Seabury Press, 1979), p. 52.
2. Alan Richardson, *The Theological Word Book of the Bible*, (London: Camelot Press Ltd., 1950), p. 143.
3. *The Book of Common Prayer*, p. 379.
4. ibid, pp. 94, 95.
5. ibid, p. 302.
6. Kenneth McAll, *Healing the Family Tree*, (London: Sheldon Press, 1982), p. 121,122.

Nine: Deliverance During Healing of Generations

1. *Deliverance Highlights*, (cassettes or video), Christian Healing Ministries, P. O. Box 9520, Jacksonville, FL 32208.

Ten: God is Raising an Army!

1. **The Book of Common Prayer**, 1928 p. 280.
2. Henri Nouwen, *Out of Solitude*, (Notre Dame: Ave Maria Press, 1974), p. 40. ·
3. *The Book of Common Prayer*, p. 236
4. Nouwen, p. 22.
5. Jeanne Guyon, *Experiencing the Depths of Jesus Christ*, (Auburn, ME: SeedSowers Christian Books, 1975), p. 1.
6. Anthony Bloom and Georges LeFebvre, *Courage to Pray*, (New York: Paulist Press, 1973), p. 55.

Appendix C: Scriptural Foundations

1. *The Book of Common Prayer*, p. 862.
2. ibid, p. 862.
3. ibid, p. 96.
4. *The Interpreter's Bible, Volume XII*, pp. 132,133. Copyright 1957 by Abingdon Press. Used by permission.

Appendix E

Related Reading

John H. Hampsch, C.M.F., *Healing Your Family Tree*, Indiana: Our Sunday Visitor, Inc., 1989.

Matthew Linn, S.J., Dennis Linn, S.J., Sheila Fabricant, *Healing the Greatest Hurt*, New Jersey: Paulist, 1985.

Francis MacNutt, *Deliverance from Evil Spirits*, Michigan: Chosen Books, 1995.

Dr. Kenneth McAll, *Healing the Family Tree*, London: Sheldon Press, 1982.
...*Healing the Haunted*, London: Darley Anderson, 1989.
...*A Guide to Healing the Family Tree*, Carberry, Scotland: The Handsel Press, Ltd.

Derek Prince, *Blessing or Curse*, New York: Chosen Books, 1990.

Agnes Sanford, *The Healing Light*, New York: Ballantine Books, 1972.

John & Paula Sandford, *Healing the Wounded Spirit*, New Jersey: Bridge Publishing, Inc., 1985.
...*The Transformation of the Inner Man*, New Jersey: Bridge Publishing, Inc., 1982.

David Watson, *The Hidden Battle*, Illinois, Harold Shaw Publishers, 1980.

Book and Tape Order Forms

[Newsletter: *Setting the Wounded Free* included with each order.]

Copies of *From Generation to Generation: A Manual for Ministry* and cassette tapes may be ordered directly by filling out and mailing the coupon below. The following tapes are available:

Set A - Healing of Memories: Set of 5 - $30. One tape - $7.

    Tape 1: Healing of Memories: Our Need and God's Response
    Tape 2: Prenatal Prayer
    Tape 3: Healing Our Losses, Great and Small
    Tape 4: God Wants Our Families Whole!
    Tape 5: Healing of Generations (Introductory)

Set B - Healing of Generations: Set of 6 - $36. One tape - $7.

    Tape 1: An Ancient Connection: Intro. to Healing of Generations
    Tape 2: The Transformation of Time
    Tape 3: Root Causes of Present Day Problems
    Tape 4: I. Steps to Healing of Generations
    Tape 5: II. Steps to Healing of Generations
    Tape 6: The Holy Eucharist of the Generations

Please send the following items:

#____*From Generation to Generation, A Manual for Ministry* - $10.95

Circle tapes wanted: Set I: 1 2 3 4 5   Set II: 1 2 3 4 5 6

Name_____Street

Address_____

City_____ State ____ Zip Code _____

Please add .07% sales tax for items shipped to Florida addresses.
Shipping: Books: $2.50 for first, plus .75 cents for each additional book. Air Mail $3.50 per book.
Tapes: $2.50 per tape, $3.50 per set.
(Note: Surface shipping may take two to three weeks.)

Send this coupon, with check for payment, plus shipping and handling charges to:

Jehovah Rapha Press
P. O. Box 14780
Jacksonville, FL 32238-1780

Book and Tape Order Forms

[Newsletter: *Setting the Wounded Free* included with each order.]

Copies of *From Generation to Generation: A Manual for Ministry* and cassette tapes can be ordered directly by filling out and mailing the coupon below. The following tapes are available:

Set A - Healing of Memories: Set of 5 - $30. One tape - $7.

>   Tape 1: Healing of Memories: Our Need and God's Response
>   Tape 2: Prenatal Prayer
>   Tape 3: Healing Our Losses, Great and Small
>   Tape 4: God Wants Our Families Whole!
>   Tape 5: Healing of Generations (Introductory)

Set B - Healing of Generations: Set of 6 - $36. One tape - $7.

>   Tape 1: An Ancient Connection: Intro. to Healing of Generations
>   Tape 2: The Transformation of Time
>   Tape 3: Root Causes of Present Day Problems
>   Tape 4: I. Steps to Healing of Generations
>   Tape 5: II. Steps to Healing of Generations
>   Tape 6: The Holy Eucharist of the Generations

Please send the following items:

#____ *From Generation to Generation, A Manual for Ministry* - $10.95

Circle tapes wanted to order: Set I: 1 2 3 4 5   Set II: 1 2 3 4 5 6

Name_____Street

Address_____

City_____ State____ Zip Code_____

Please add .07% sales tax for items shipped to Florida addresses.
Shipping: Books: $2.50 for first, plus .75 cents for each additional book. Air Mail $3.50 per book.
Tapes: $2.50 per tape, $3.50 per set.
(Note: Surface shipping may take two to three weeks.)

Send this coupon, with check for payment, plus shipping and handling charges to:

Jehovah Rapha Press
P.O.Box 14780
Jacksonville, FL 32238-1780

Book and Tape Order Forms

[Newsletter: *Setting the Wounded Free* included with each order.]

Copies of *From Generation to Generation: A Manual for Ministry* and cassette tapes may be ordered directly by filling out and mailing the coupon below. The following tapes are available:

Set A - Healing of Memories: Set of 5 - $30. One tape - $7.

    Tape 1: Healing of Memories: Our Need and God's Response
    Tape 2: Prenatal Prayer
    Tape 3: Healing Our Losses, Great and Small
    Tape 4: God Wants Our Families Whole!
    Tape 5: Healing of Generations (Introductory)

Set B - Healing of Generations: Set of 6 - $36. One tape - $7.

    Tape 1: An Ancient Connection: Intro. to Healing of Generations
    Tape 2: The Transformation of Time
    Tape 3: Root Causes of Present Day Problems
    Tape 4: I. Steps to Healing of Generations
    Tape 5: II. Steps to Healing of Generations
    Tape 6: The Holy Eucharist of the Generations

Please send the following items:

#____*From Generation to Generation, A Manual for Ministry* - $10.95

Circle tapes wanted: Set I: 1 2 3 4 5   Set II: 1 2 3 4 5 6

Name_____Street

Address_____

City_____   State   Zip Code_____

Please add .07% sales tax for items shipped to Florida addresses.
Shipping: Books: $2.50 for first, plus .75 cents for each additional book. Air Mail $3.50 per book.
Tapes: $2.50 per tape, $3.50 per set.
(Note: Surface shipping may take two to three weeks.)

Send this coupon, with check for payment, plus shipping and handling charges to:

Jehovah Rapha Press
P. O. Box 14780
Jacksonville, FL 32238-1780